Practical Teaching
A Guide to Assessment and Quality Assurance

Linda Wilson

✦ CENGAGE
Learning·

Australia • Brazil • Japan • Korea • Mexico • Singapore • Spain • United Kingdom • United States

CENGAGE
Learning®

Practical Teaching: A Guide to Assessment and Quality Assurance

Linda Wilson

Publishing Director: Linden Harris

Commissioning Editor: Lucy Mills

Development Editor: Helen Green

Production Editor: Alison Cooke

Production Controller: Eyvett Davis

Marketing Manager: Lauren Mottram

Typesetter: MPS Limited, a Macmillan Company

Cover design: Adam Renvoize

Printed in China by RR Donnelley

1 2 3 4 5 6 7 8 9 10–14 13 12

© 2012 Cengage Learning EMEA

For product information and technology assistance, contact: **emea.info@cengage.com.**

For permission to use material from this text or product, and for permission queries, email emea.permissions@cengage.com.

British Library Cataloguing-in-Publication Data
A catalogue record for this book is available from the British Library.

ISBN: 978-1-4080-4861-0

Cengage Learning EMEA
Cheriton House, North Way, Andover, Hampshire, SP10 5BE, United Kingdom

Cengage Learning products are represented in Canada by Nelson Education Ltd.

For your lifelong learning solutions, visit
www.cengage.co.uk

Purchase your next print book, e-book or e-chapter at
www.cengagebrain.com

Brief contents

Contents

Introduction

I have been involved in assessment and verification since the late 1980s. I have seen many mutations of training programmes, terminology and qualifications, and this is my opportunity to put onto paper helpful hints and identify potential pitfalls for new or inexperienced assessors and quality assurance staff. I hope that the teachers and trainers of assessors and quality assurance staff will also find the activities useful in developing skills and delivering their courses. To date there are very few texts that focus entirely on assessment and quality assurance and fewer that link so clearly to the National Occupational Standards and the new qualifications.

The book is aimed at those wishing to achieve their assessor or internal quality assurance award – the candidate assessors or candidate quality assurers. Some aspects of the book also support the trainers of the qualifications. Chapter 1 The principles of assessment: functions and concepts and Chapter 2 Planning and delivering assessments are concerned with assessment; Chapter 3 Quality assurance of assessment and Chapter 4 Internally assuring the quality of assessment are related to quality assurance and Chapter 5 Managing the quality assurance process is directed at those managing the processes. Chapter 6 Collecting evidence and compiling a portfolio aims to put all the learning together and summarise how candidates might evidence their competence.

The structure of the chapters

Each chapter commences with a clear set of learning outcomes, which are reviewed at the end of the chapter together with a summary of how they were achieved. The content of each chapter is linked to the assessment criteria of the assessment and quality assurance qualifications.

The chapters, which are written in a user friendly manner, include a range of theoretical concepts and practical applications. Throughout the chapters activities, watch points and case studies guide the reader to develop their understanding of the subject. Each concludes with a list of specialist terminology and key words with references to further reading on the topics.

The terminology used in the sector is varied. To clarify, in this edition, candidates are those working towards qualifications (apprentices, trainees, learners, students, etc.).

You will see many references to quality assurance and quality assurer throughout the book. For ease of referencing quality assurance has been given the acronym QA and quality assurer has been written out in full. However quality assurance and quality assurer are interchangeable and if required can be used as such.

The subject matter

Practical Teaching: A Guide to Assessment and Quality Assurance is my third book in a series of teachers' texts relating to the current National Occupational Standards for the sector. This particular book maps directly to the City and Guilds Assessment and Quality Assurance (6317) qualifications. The former relate to teacher training qualifications – PTLLS, CTLLS and DTLLS and are proving to be a valuable help to trainee teachers.

The assessor and quality assurance qualifications are the new generation of assessor and internal verifier (IV) qualifications, the former versions being informally known as the D units (expired in 2002) and more recently the A & V units (expired December 2010). The first noticeable change, therefore, is the change of expression from internal verifier to quality assurance staff. This reflects the broader role of the verifier, which in the new awards includes moderation and other quality assurance processes. At this point it should be noted that holders of those former qualifications do not need to re-qualify, although they may use the new assessor and quality assurance awards to update the currency of their skills. The new units would make ideal continuous professional development opportunities.

Ofqual stated in 2010 that there is no mandatory requirement to re-qualify, re-train or upskill to the Assessment and Quality Assurance units. However, all centres must ensure that all their assessors and internal quality assurance staff (IQAs previously known as IVs) – irrespective of sector – are working in line with the March 2010 National Occupational Standards (NOS) for Learning and Development.

www.cityandguilds.com

What are they?

They are a series of units of assessment which when clustered together form awards and certificates within the qualifications credit framework. The tables below relate to the qualifications accredited by City and Guilds. Other awarding organisations take the National Occupational Standards and units of assessment (from Lifelong Learning UK) and then make their own qualifications. Each has to go through the same rigorous accreditation so are comparable with each other. They are valid in England, Wales and Northern Ireland. A different set of qualifications is applicable to Scottish assessors and verifiers. At launch, the qualifications were known as the Training, Assessment and Quality Assurance qualifications with an expectation that further qualifications around training will follow.

Qualification clusters – assessment

The table below lists the titles and reference numbers for each qualification, the units of assessment that make up each qualification, the credit value of each unit of assessment on the Qualification Credit Framework (QCF) and the required Guided Learning Hours (GLH) for each qualification.

Title	C&G Code	Units		QCF value	GLH
Level 3 Award Understanding the Principles and Practices of assessment	6317-30	●	Understanding the principles and practices of assessment	3 credits	24
Level 3 Award Assessing Competence in the Work Environment	6317-31	●	Understanding the principles and practices of assessment	3 credits	54
		●	Assess occupational competence in the work environment	6 credits	

Title	C&G Code	Units	QCF value	GLH
Level 3 Award Assessing Vocationally Related Achievement	6317-32	• Understanding the principles and practices of assessment • Assessing vocational skills, knowledge and understanding	3 credits 6 credits	54
Level 3 Certificate Assessing Vocational Achievement	6317-33	• Understanding the principles and practices of assessment • Assess occupational competence in the work environment • Assessing vocational skills, knowledge and understanding	3 credits 6 credits 6 credits	84

Qualification clusters – quality assurance

Title	C&G Code	Units	QCF value	GLH
Level 4 Award Understanding the Internal Quality Assurance of Assessment Processes and Practice	6317-40	• Understanding the principles and practices of internally assuring the quality of assessment	6 credits	45
Level 4 Award Internal Quality Assurance of Assessment Processes and Practice	6317-41	• Understanding the principles and practices of internally assuring the quality of assessment • Internally assure the quality of assessment	6 credits 6 credits	90

Title	C&G Code	Units		QCF value	GLH
Level 4 Certificate Leading the Internal Quality Assurance of Assessment Processes and Practice	6317-42	●	Understanding the principles and practices of internally assuring the quality of assessment	6 credits	115
		●	Internally assure the quality of assessment	6 credits	
		●	Plan, allocate and monitor work in own area of responsibility	5 credits	

So what's changed?

Well the qualification framework has for one. The old qualifications were written against the National Qualifications Framework (NQF) and needed to be rewritten aligning the qualifications to the Qualifications Credit Framework (QCF). This was quite timely given the age of the former qualifications.

Change	Old	New
Written against QCF with credit values and different sizes of qualifications	No	Yes
Knowledge and understanding inclusive in qualifications	Inherent	Mandatory, stand-alone units
Practical assessments	Yes	Yes
Work based assessor routes (pathways)	Generic in (A2)	Bespoke in-service practical units
Vocational assessor routes (pathways)	Yes in (A1)	Bespoke in-service practical units
Suitability for all assessors/quality assurance staff	NVQ only	All assessors and quality assurers

Change	Old	New
Suitable for those working with accredited or non-accredited learning programmes or work based training	No	Yes
Units for aspiring assessors or QA staff or non-practitioners	No	Stand-alone knowledge units
Links to other qualifications, e.g. teaching qualifications	No	Potential RPL
Suitable for those managing or co-ordinating QA process	No	Yes
Assessor Awards and Certificates at Level 3	Yes	Yes
Quality Assurance (Internal Verifier) Awards and Certificates at Level 4	Yes	Yes
Unit Accreditation	Yes	Yes
Holistic assessment available	No	Yes

Who can do them?

The qualifications are suitable for those who work, or want to work, as:

- Assessors/teachers/trainers/tutors in the Lifelong Learning Sector or Adult/Community Education.
- Assessors/trainers of personnel in commerce, industry, public and voluntary sectors or HM Forces.
- Quality assurance/internal verifiers and support staff in Further and Adult Education.
- Quality assurance managers and internal verifiers in workplace training and further and adult education.

The qualifications are suitable provided that assessors are qualified in the subject they intend to assess by virtue of holding an appropriate professional qualification or employed in a training/teaching role. The decision as to what constitutes an appropriate qualification is at the discretion of the training provider or employer (City & Guilds: http://www.cityandguilds.com website, accessed June 2011).

This book seeks to summarise effective strategies in assessment and quality assurance. I hope that new assessors and quality assurers will find it helpful as they gain their skills and develop their competence.

Acknowledgements

I would like to take this opportunity to thank my reviewers, City and Guilds and the staff at Cengage. In particular, John, who once again offered his experience, opinions and support during its preparation.

The author's previous books, published by Cengage Learning are:

Practical Teaching: A Guide to PTLLS and CTLLS (2008)

Practical Teaching: A Guide to PTLLS and DTLLS (2009)

Walk-through tour

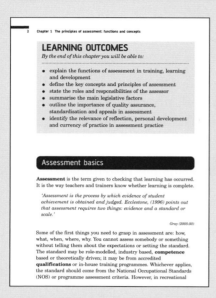

Learning outcomes Featured at the beginning of each chapter, you can check at a glance what you are about to learn

Case study Practical, real-world examples illustrate key points and learning objectives in the text

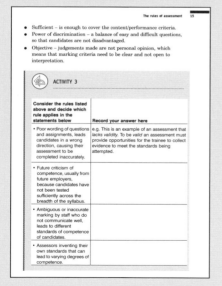

Activity Put your knowledge into action with these practical activities

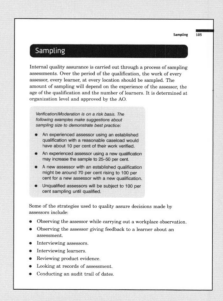

Note box Key information is drawn out in eye-catching boxes

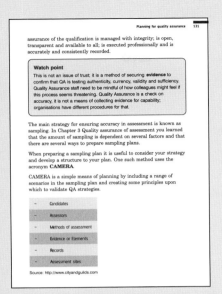

Watch point Useful hints and tips to alert assessors or IQA staff of potential challenges

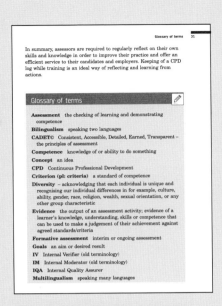

Glossary of terms Glossary of terms highlighted in the text are listed at the end of each chapter with definitions

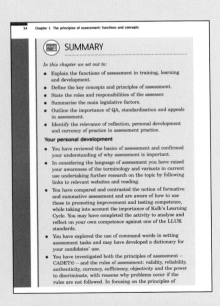

Summary Featured at the end of each chapter, summary boxes help you to consolidate what you have learned

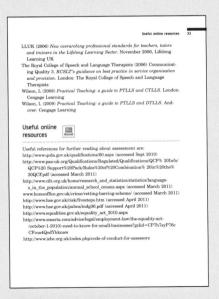

Useful resources Further reading feature offers suggestions for print and online reading material

CHAPTER 1

The principles of assessment: functions and concepts

Unit of Assessment	Assessment Criteria
Understanding the principles and practices of assessment	1.1; 1.2; 1.3; 1.4; 6.1; 6.2; 6.3; 8.1; 8.3; 8.4
Assess occupational competence in the work environment	2.3; 3.3; 4.1; 4.2; 4.3; 4.4
Assess vocational skills, knowledge and understanding	2.5; 3.3; 4.1; 4.2; 4.3; 4.4
Understanding the principles and practices of internally assuring the quality of assessment	No direct references
Internally assure the quality of assessment	No direct references
Plan, allocate and monitor work in own area of responsibility	No direct references

LEARNING OUTCOMES

By the end of this chapter you will be able to:

- explain the functions of assessment in training, learning and development
- define the key concepts and principles of assessment
- state the roles and responsibilities of the assessor
- summarise the main legislative factors
- outline the importance of quality assurance, standardisation and appeals in assessment
- identify the relevance of reflection, personal development and currency of practice in assessment practice

Assessment basics

Assessment is the term given to checking that learning has occurred. It is the way teachers and trainers know whether learning is complete.

> *'Assessment is the process by which evidence of student achievement is obtained and judged. Ecclestone, (1996) points out that assessment requires two things: evidence and a standard or scale.'*

> *Gray (2005:50)*

Some of the first things you need to grasp in assessment are: how, what, when, where, why. You cannot assess somebody or something without telling them about the expectations or setting the standard. The standard may be role-modelled, industry based, **competence** based or theoretically driven; it may be from accredited **qualifications** or in-house training programmes. Whichever applies, the standard should come from the National Occupational Standards (NOS) or programme assessment criteria. However, in recreational provision there are unlikely to be such formal **standards**, so the standard becomes the teacher's, employer's and/or the candidate's **goals**. Therefore, standards and goals are the keys to successful assessment.

> **Watch point**
>
> If you know where you are going, you'll be able to tell when you've got there.

The output of assessment is 'evidence'; **evidence** is the confirmation that assessment has occurred and the way it is proven. To summarise, assessment is a 'method of confirming learning'.

Why assess?

Businesses and training institutions are driven by the need to have a qualified workforce. In both the private and public sectors this need is met through a range of opportunities delivered either on their premises or in conjunction with a college or private training provider. Education and training is delivered as part of a professional development programme, apprenticeship, day-release or full-time education programme. Whichever way the education or training is delivered there is a need to ensure that the standards are consistent and recognisable. To this end each occupational sector (see Appendix A Occupational sectors – Sector subject areas (SSA)) has a series of qualifications. Where qualifications do not exist, perhaps because the employer has their own specific training needs, there is still a need to produce standards by which to measure learning.

The need for assessment is, therefore, linked to national or organisational standards. Assessment is required to ensure the integrity of those standards.

The language of assessment

The terminology or language of assessment leads to the introduction of words which demand further explanation. This section introduces the reader to the technical language of assessment.

Assessment can be carried out before recruitment (at interview), at commencement (diagnostic and initial assessment), during and at the end of the learning or training activity and at the end of the module, unit or programme. It may be pertinent at this point to look at how qualifications are structured, as this will lead us to the points at which assessment should occur.

Programme of study

A collection of qualifications which create an apprenticeship framework, a college course or training programme. Also described as a curriculum.

In September 2010 a new qualifications framework was launched. As with the previous National Qualifications Framework (NQF), the Qualifications Credit Framework (QCF) lists a hierarchy of levels of qualifications. In the new system, a tariff was issued with eight levels of qualification of increasing difficulty. These levels meant that qualifications could be matched against each other – for example at Level 3 you will be able to undertake an A level, an Advanced Apprenticeship or a BTEC Extended Diploma. While they will be different sizes within the Level 3, they all have parity in terms of difficulty. Figure 1.1 shows the QCF.

In the vocational sector, NOS are written by the Sector Skills Councils (SSCs). These standards form the basis of the **units of assessment** and the resultant qualifications created by awarding organisations.

Qualification

A certificated qualification, endorsed by an awarding organisation and approved through the Qualifications and Credit Framework (QCF, see www.ofqual.gov.uk for more information).

For example, some qualifications you may come across include:

Entry   Functional Skills Mathematics

Level 1   NVQ Diploma in Hairdressing and Beauty Therapy (QCF)

Level 2   Certificate in Health and Social Care (QCF)

Figure 1.1 The Qualifications Credit Framework

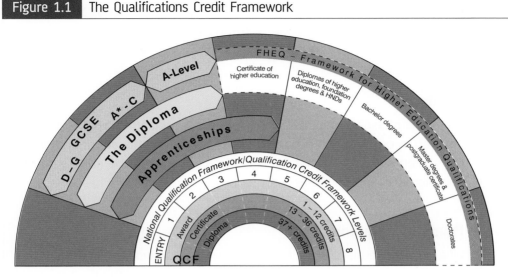

Source: Ofqual, August 2011.

Level 3 Extended Diploma in Public Services (Uniformed) (QCF)

Level 4 Certificate in Teaching in the Lifelong Learning Sector

Level 5 HND Diploma in Business (QCF)

A qualification consists of a number of units of assessment, clustered to create a certificated qualification.

Units of assessment

The smaller subsections of the qualification which focus on a particular aspect of the subject. There will usually be several units in a qualification.

Each unit will have its own specified learning outcomes and assessment criteria. Each will have a specified level and credit value. Additional information may be provided to guide the assessment process. The documentation will also state the name of the sector skills area which owns the unit. In some qualifications, units of assessment from different sector areas will be combined to create meaningful qualifications.

Content

Each unit of assessment will have statements relating to what has to be covered in order to achieve the unit. These statements about content are written in terms of what the candidate will know or be able to do on completion of the unit of assessment.

Rules of combination

Qualifications consist of mandatory and optional units. As their names infer, mandatory units are those which must be achieved and optional ones are usually from a list of units arranged singularly or in groups from which the candidate must select a specified number. The purpose of grouping units is to ensure that qualifications contain the range of competence expected in the industry.

Version 4 http://www.paa-uk.org/Qualifications/Regulated/Qualifications/QCF%20Info/QCF%20Support%20Pack/Rules%20of%20Combination%20in%20the%20QCF.pdf (accessed July 2011)

Accumulation and transfer of credits

In order to provide benchmarks for qualifications, the regulatory body **Ofqual** requires that each unit in a set of NOS is set at a *level* of learning. This determines the level of difficulty of the unit. It varies from entry (entry 1, entry 2 and entry 3), through level 1 to level 8. Level 2 is roughly equivalent to GCSE level and level 3 equivalent to A level standard, whereas, level 8 is PhD standard (see Figure 1.1 above). Another benchmark is that of *size*. This refers to the volume of learning and is stated as a 'credit'; an award comprises 1 to 12 credits; a certificate comprises 13 to 36 credits; a diploma comprises of 37 credits or more.

> **Watch point**
> This change is different to the earlier framework in which a diploma was at a higher level than a certificate. Now there are awards, certificates and diplomas at all levels; they are now determined by their size, not their difficulty.

The final benchmark relates to *subject*; qualifications are categorised into the subject sector classification scheme. For example, Assessor and Quality Assurance units are in subject area 13 – Education and Training, sector area 13.2 – Direct Learning Support.

Programmes of learning and apprenticeships are arranged around these frameworks; you may be employed to deliver a particular unit or module or you may work within a team of people who train towards a whole or part qualification. Whichever strategy is used, the teacher or trainer will have to assess that learning has occurred. In some qualifications this learning is referred to as 'demonstrating competence'.

Term	Alternative expressions
Qualification	Standards, specifications, course, syllabus, programme, apprenticeship written by an awarding organisation following a set of NOS
Learning outcome	Objective, range statements, content, statements of competence
Evidence requirements	Assessment guidance, evidence, portfolio, assignment, assessment criteria
Grading	Grading criteria are the level at which the outcomes are met – e.g. pass merit/credit or distinction
Quality assurance (QA)	Verification, moderation, standardisation
Assessment	Test, exam, evidence (proof)

Unfortunately, assessment is such a wide topic and the qualification frameworks are so varied that there are many different terms used (assessment jargon) and it sometimes takes a while to learn the terminology; usually when you do discover their meaning it is broadly the same as another similar term used in a different qualification team. Let us look at some of those terms.

Command words

Within every set of units of assessment, there are a series of statements to define exactly what a candidate has to do in order to demonstrate their competence against a specific set of standards.

For example: 'explain …' is frequently seen. Explain can be defined as 'to make something clear by giving a detailed account of relevant facts or circumstances'. How a candidate does this will be 'explained' in Chapter 2, but suffice to say, at this point, it could be written, verbal, demonstrated, or a combination of those strategies. It is the skill of the assessor that will guide the candidate towards an effective method.

 ACTIVITY 1

Make a list of command words you use in your training or learning environment when 'explaining' the subject or how it will be assessed.

Consider:

Wording in assignments or instructions to complete question sheets.

e.g.: explain   *

*   *

*   *

*   *

Extension activity:

Create a dictionary of terms that your candidates may find helpful.

Clue: look at the learning outcomes in a qualification. Sentences usually start with a word that indicates what needs to be done in order to meet the requirements of the outcome. Awarding organisations also have resources to explain their command words.

Concepts of assessment

A **concept** is an idea, in this instance, about assessment. The concepts that you will commonly see are: **criterion** referencing; **formative assessment** and **summative assessment**.

Criterion referencing When a candidate (trainee, learner, student) achieves a standard, they either can (or can't) do the task, answer the question or demonstrate competence. They can continue in their attempts until the criterion is achieved (plural is criteria). Therefore in this style of assessment the assessor is measuring what a candidate can do. While it is generally associated with a 'can do–can't do' (pass–fail) assessment, it may be linked to a grading scale which determines how well a candidate can do something. In this strategy a candidate can pass, pass with merit or pass with distinction.

 ACTIVITY 2

Assess your own performance against the statements of competence:

If you were to measure your performance as a teacher or trainer against the 'New overarching professional standards for teachers, tutors and trainers in the lifelong learning sector' (LLUK, 2006), you would be undertaking an assessment using criteria. For example, this is an extract from Domain E – Assessment for Learning, using criteria related to professional practice (LLUK, 2006: p11–12). By comparing your status against the standard you can complete the self-assessment.

	Standard	How do you measure up to the standard? Do you do this? How? What evidence do you have to prove this?
EP1.1	Use appropriate forms of assessment and evaluate their effectiveness in producing information useful to the teacher and the learner	
EP1.2	Devise, select, use and appraise assessment tools, including where appropriate, those which exploit new and emerging technologies	
EP2.1	Apply appropriate methods of assessment fairly and effectively	
EP2.3	Design appropriate assessment activities for own specialist area	
EP3.2	Ensure that access to assessment is appropriate to learner need	
EP4.2	Use feedback to evaluate and improve own skills in assessment	
EP5.3	Communicate relevant assessment information to those with a legitimate interest in learner achievement, as necessary/appropriate	

In the boxes on the right you will have written statements, made lists, justified your choices and opinions, described strategies and given examples of instances when the competence is demonstrated. As this is a self-assessment, and therefore only an individual's opinion of their ability, the judgements will usually be supported by other assessments.

The units in the assessment and quality assurance qualification also base assessment decisions on criteria (see Appendix B Units of assessment (City & Guilds)). They are different to the LLUK (2006) criteria. It is important, therefore, not to muddle criteria contained within different awards or sets of standards.

Formative assessment An interim judgement, also known as 'continuous assessment'. It has the advantage of being an ideal opportunity to tell a candidate how they are progressing and giving them the chance to improve. This type of assessment is highly motivational because it is seen as a review rather than an assessment. It helps candidates to progress and maximise their potential. There is life after formative assessment! One of the disadvantages of formative assessment (although significantly outweighed by the advantages) is that continuous assessment may feel like *continual* assessment. Kolb's learning cycle (see Figure 1.2) advocates the concepts of formative assessment and feedback clearly within the cycle, indicating their value in personal development and progression. Formative assessment aids learning.

Figure 1.2   Kolb's learning cycle (1984)

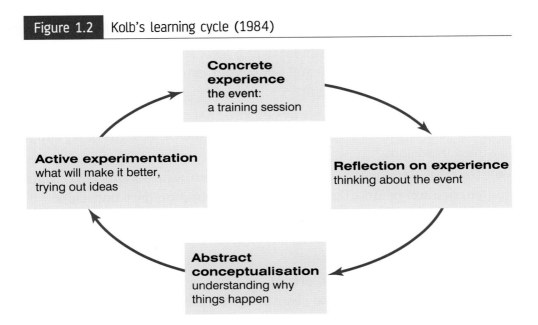

Summative assessment The form of assessment usually associated with tests and exams. It aids the assessment of learning and is a formal process to close a stage of learning or training; thus enabling the whole programme to move forward. In summative assessment styles, a candidate progresses through their qualification or unit of study until the time comes that learning is complete and they are tested on their knowledge or skills. A judgement is made, which is then expressed on a certificate. If a candidate wishes to improve they usually have to 'sit' the examination again. This does put enormous pressure on candidates as the outcomes may determine their future. However, with teaching that prepares a candidate well for their test, such apprehension and anxiety can be lessened. In a less formal situation the summative assessment is usually completed in smaller chunks to build up to the whole qualification. This is where formative and summative concepts overlap and the meaning of the terminology becomes less black and white.

Principles of assessment

A **principle** is a rule that you will follow; it is an underlying standard that you will not compromise. Some of the principles that you should advocate are:

- Consistency – you will always ensure that the methods and timeliness of your assessment is at a level standard, making certain that irrespective of how and when your candidates are assessed, the outcomes are constant.
- Accessibility – you will always ensure that all of your candidates are able to access your assessments and follow systems of equality and inclusion.
- Detailed – you will always ensure that your assessments cover your curriculum or unit fairly and evenly, leaving no part undecided.
- Earned – you will always ensure that your candidates have achieved their qualifications with rigour and others will respect the integrity of the assessment.
- Transparency – you will always ensure that everyone involved in the assessment is crystal clear about its purpose and meaning.

These principles form the acronym **CADET©**:

C	Consistent
A	Accessible
D	Detailed
E	Earned
T	Transparent

So, these are the values and principles that you follow when preparing, implementing and evaluating assessment. It will be these values that will help to determine the effectiveness of your assessment.

It should be remembered that assessment is not merely something which occurs in the workplace or end of year test. In every training session that you do you will set learning outcomes, deliver your topic and then close the session. You must remember that to truly know if you have achieved the learning outcomes you must set an assessment activity. If the close of your session is: 'Is everybody OK with that?' you may be able to claim that you have 'taught' your topic, but you cannot claim that your candidates have learned anything! You must, therefore, include into the structure of your training session, small assessment activities which help you to confirm learning. The easiest to prepare are verbal or written questions – but make sure everyone contributes and remember that you can use similar activities in the follow up session as a recap activity, before moving forward to the next topic. In the next chapter we will review the different ways that this can be achieved.

The rules of assessment

Once you have sorted out the basics of assessment, you can get down to the actual assessment. There are a number of different ways of assessing, but all rely on the fact that you need something to measure against. These are usually written by awarding organisations but there are some courses where you may have to devise your own standards, for example non-qualification courses, industry training schemes or recreational programmes.

> ## Watch point
>
> NEVER substitute your own standards onto qualifications which are approved within the QCF, however well intentioned.

Qualifications are written against NOS and approved as such by organisations charged with the remit to create a standard across the country, e.g. City & Guilds. If you change the specifications contained in the qualifications you will disadvantage your candidates, because you are creating your own qualification, which will not be recognised within your professional area. A similar rule should apply to the delivery of industry training courses; these courses are agreed at head office level and provide a standard across the company.

The first task when planning assessment is to gain sight of the awarding organisation's specifications for your unit/module or qualification. In it you will find a series of paragraphs telling you what a candidate will:

- know
- be able to do
- demonstrate,

at the end of the unit or module.

Some qualifications/units will tell you that you need to collect two of this, a report on that, or an observation for the other. But more often it will be up to you to decide on the appropriate assessment task and the method, usually under the supervision of the Internal Quality Assurer (**IQA**). There are some **rules** that will help you make informed choices. You should ensure that your assessments are:

- Valid/relevant – assesses what it is supposed to, according to the curriculum, in an appropriate manner.
- Reliable/fair – assesses in a consistent manner to the expected standards, regardless of who makes the judgement or when the judgement is made without any bias or preference.
- Authentic – is able to be attributed to the candidate.
- Current/recent – is up to date and recently written.

- Sufficient – is enough to cover the content/performance criteria.
- Power of discrimination – a balance of easy and difficult questions, so that candidates are not disadvantaged.
- Objective – judgements made are not personal opinion, which means that marking criteria need to be clear and not open to interpretation.

ACTIVITY 3

Consider the rules listed above and decide which rule applies in the statements below	Record your answer here
• Poor wording of questions and assignments, leads candidates in a wrong direction, causing their assessment to be completed inaccurately.	e.g. This is an example of an assessment that *lacks validity*. To be *valid* an assessment must provide opportunities for the trainee to collect evidence to meet the standards being attempted.
• Future criticism of competence, usually from future employers, because candidates have not been tested sufficiently across the breadth of the syllabus.	
• Ambiguous or inaccurate marking by staff who do not communicate well, leads to different standards of competence of candidates.	
• Assessors inventing their own standards that can lead to varying degrees of competence.	

Consider the rules listed above and decide which rule applies in the statements below	Record your answer here
• Poor research skills leading to inaccurate citation and/or plagiarism.	
• Work presented in a portfolio is not signed or dated.	

To overcome these issues, you should follow the rules of assessment, by:

● Always ensuring that your candidates are prepared for their assessments.

● Devising tasks that test what you have taught.

● Telling candidates how, when and where assessments will happen.

● Offering study skills to support presentation of research in work.

● Asking colleagues (or IQA) to review the task before submitting to candidates (when devising assessments).

● Creating varied assessment tasks to give good coverage of material and opportunities for differentiation.

The role and responsibilities of the assessor

To develop an understanding of the role of the assessor, it is helpful first to consider who else is involved in an assessment. The key roles of people involved in the assessment process starts with the candidate who is assessed by the assessor who then submits work to the quality assurer (QA). This simplistic process is further explained as:

Title	Role	May also be known as:
Candidate	To attend regularly To achieve award in a timely manner To respect the rules of the organisation	Trainee, learner, student
Trainer	To demonstrate skills To teach underpinning knowledge (UPK) To raise confidence To monitor progress towards assessment	Tutor, teacher, coach, facilitator
Skills assessor	To make judgements about skills, usually in the work environment To ask oral questions to test knowledge related to the task To check validity, currency, authenticity and sufficiency of evidence To feedback the outcome of assessment To make records To process assessments to the QA stage	Assessor, first line assessor, trainer, observer
UPK assessor	To make judgements about knowledge and understanding To check validity, currency, authenticity and sufficiency of evidence To feedback the outcome of assessment To make records To process assessments to the QA stage	Assessor, second line assessor, teacher

▶

Title	Role	May also be known as:
IQA	To confirm that assessments are valid, current, authentic and sufficient to meet the assessment criteria To support and guide assessors To make records To lead on standardisation activities To plan external QA visits To liaise with awarding organisations	Internal verifier (**IV**) Internal moderator (**IM**)
External quality assurer	Appointed by the awarding organisation To confirm assessment and QA procedures comply with awarding organisation assessment guidance	External verifier External moderator External examiner

The assessor will work with the candidate in the following ways:

- Providing initial advice and guidance prior to enrolment.
- Preparing and delivering an induction to the programme, qualification and organisation.
- Undertaking initial assessment to ascertain the best **pathway**.
- Undertaking diagnostic assessment to check or confirm previous learning.
- Identifying additional learning requirements.
- Introducing the candidate to the framework or qualification.
- Preparing the programme of study and long- and short-term targets.
- Providing a platform for learning – a trainer may do this.
- Planning assessments.
- Reviewing targets and progress.
- Undertaking a range of assessment activities according to need.

- Supporting and advising the candidate on methods of collecting evidence to support competence.
- Giving feedback to the candidate.
- Confirming validity, sufficiency, authenticity and currency of evidence.
- Keeping records of assessment.

In addition, the assessor is required to participate in QA processes, many of which are described briefly later in this chapter or in detail in Chapter 3 Quality assurance of assessment and Chapter 4 Internally assuring the quality of assessment:

- Be the first point of contact between the candidate and the QA.
- Contribute to QA procedures.
- Attend standardisation activities.
- Fully understand the qualification.
- Maintain and update own expertise and professional development.
- Maintain own licence to practice.

The qualities the assessor will possess include:

- Organisational skills.
- Time management skills.
- Patience.
- Communication skills.
- The ability to evaluate/assess objectively and accurately against units of assessment and NOS.
- An approachable manner within boundaries of role.
- Perception.
- The ability to judge without appearing to interrogate or sanction.
- An ability to create relationships built on trust and integrity.
- Knowledge of systems and procedures and the ability to be the 'guardian of the rules'.
- Advocacy of high standards.

Legislation

This section covers the main items of legislation covering the assessment and QA roles. It should be read within those parameters. Every assessor will also be occupationally competent in their field of expertise and, therefore, will need to be aware of the legislation pertinent to their subject.

Health and Safety at Work Act 1974

Everyone has a responsibility for the safety of themselves and others, therefore, rules must be followed and safe practices adhered to. You should demonstrate a model of best practice, lead by example. There are additional rules relating to taking candidates on educational visits following a series of tragic accidents. Do not consider taking candidates on visits without seeking advice. Health and Safety legislation requires the assessor to comply with the rules of the organisation in which their trainee is working. Assessors should wear appropriate personal protective equipment (PPE) and ensure that their trainees are compliant.

The Management of Health and Safety at Work Regulations 1999

The Regulations seek to prevent unsafe practices and minimise risk. For example: fire and emergency procedures, first aid at work, safe handling practices, visual display unit guidance and risk assessment.

Risk assessment All activities have an element of risk, some more so than others. It is the trainer/assessor's responsibility to assess the level of the risk, to establish practices to minimise risk and record such activities. The five steps to risk assessment recommended by the Health and Safety Executive (HSE) are:

   1 identify the hazards

2 decide who might be harmed and how

3 evaluate the risks and decide on the precaution

4 record the findings and implement them

5 review your assessment and update if necessary.

http://www.hse.gov.uk/risk/fivesteps.htm (accessed April 2011)

Visual display units/display screen equipment The HSE give advice to individuals and employers about working in these environments. Employees report eye strain, headaches, tiredness and discomfort, aches and repetitive strain injuries when using such equipment. The HSE advises employees to take regular short breaks to relieve eye strain, and customise chairs, desks and wrist supports to minimise discomfort and injury. The Health and Safety (Display Screen Equipment) Regulations 1992 implement an EC Directive and came into effect from January 1993 (some small changes were made in 2002). The Regulations require employers to minimise the risks in VDU work by ensuring that workplaces and jobs are well designed.

http://www.hse.gov.uk/pubns/indg36.pdf (accessed April 2011)

Child protection and safeguarding Recent high profile cases have brought about the necessity to introduce legislation and guidance on protecting children and vulnerable adults against inappropriate behaviour. Each organisation should exercise their functions with a view to safeguarding and promoting the welfare of children, (Protection of Children Act 1999, The Children Act 2004, Mental Capacity Act 2005). Mandatory Criminal Records Bureau (CRB) checks are required of anyone working closely with children and vulnerable adults. The Government holds lists of those deemed unsuitable to work with these groups and organisations should check these before appointing staff. You may also find that groups of candidates, for example child care trainees, are checked before embarking on their course of study. This is 'due diligence' on behalf of the organisation who may send these candidates into work placements in nurseries and the like.

Safeguarding is an expression which defines the broader implications of child protection as it also includes prevention. Safeguarding has been defined as:

- All agencies working with children, young people and their families taking all reasonable measures to ensure that the risks of harm to children's welfare are minimised.
- Where there are concerns about children and young people's welfare, all agencies taking appropriate actions to address those concerns, working to agreed local policies and procedures in full partnership with other local agencies.

Safeguarding Children (2005)

In February 2011 the Coalition Government published the findings of its Review into the Vetting and Barring Scheme (VBS). One of the key recommendations from the VBS review was the merging of the CRB and Independent Safeguarding Authority (ISA) to form a streamlined new body providing a proportionate barring and criminal records checking service. The guidelines require organisations to liaise with other departments in multi-agency working. This will ensure that isolated incidents collate to create a bigger picture and thus work to prevent abuse and neglect.

www.homeoffice.gov.uk/crime/vetting-barring-scheme/ (accessed March 2011)

Equality of opportunity legislation
A series of laws have been passed to ensure that no-one is discriminated against, irrespective of gender, marital status, sexual orientation, disability, race, nationality, ethnic origin, religion or belief, domestic circumstances, trade union membership, social or employment status.

For the assessor this means ensuring language, handouts and other training and learning materials are free from bias, and that inappropriate comments are challenged and excluded from the training environment. When advertising courses and delivering learning, an assessor should not stereotype or in any way disadvantage groups of candidates. The environment and all support structures should enable access and include facilities to meet all candidates' needs.

The Equality Act 2010 brings together separate pieces of legislation into one single Act simplifying the law and strengthening it in important ways to help tackle discrimination and inequality. The single equality scheme aims to meet the requirements of current legislation, which includes the following Acts, Statutory Instruments and other legislation:

- Disability Discrimination Act 1995
- Disability Equality Duty 2006
- Employment Equality (Age) Regulations 2006
- Employment Equality (Religion or Belief) Regulations 2003
- Employment Equality (Sex Discrimination) Regulations 2005
- Employment Equality (Sexual Orientation) Regulations 2003
- Equal Pay Act 1970
- Equality Act 2006
- Equality Act (Sexual Orientation) Regulations 2007
- EU Framework for Equal Treatment in Employment Directive 2000
- EU Race Discrimination Directive 2003
- Gender Equality Duty 2007
- Gender Equality Duty Code of Practice England and Wales 2006
- Gender Recognition Act 2004
- Human Rights Act 1998
- Race Relations Act 1976
- Race Relations (Amendment) Act 2000
- Sex Discrimination Act 1975
- Sex Discrimination (Gender Reassignment) Regulations 1999
- Special Educational Needs and Disability Act 2001
- Statutory Code of Practice on the Duty to Promote Race Equality 2002
- Work and Families Act 2006

Of the Acts, the following impose a duty on all public bodies to positively promote disability, race and gender equality:

- Equality Act 2006

- Disability Discrimination Act 2005
- Race Relations (Amendment) Act 2000

Government Equalities Office http://www.equalities.gov.uk/

Data protection The Data Protection Act 1998 requires any organisation that holds any data on individuals, electronic or otherwise, for more than two months, to register as data users. It restricts the sharing of data. Caution should be taken when holding records associated with candidates, staff or partner companies. It is common sense that you should never reveal personal information about anyone to another person, however convincing the request!

Duty of care Common, civil, statute and criminal law all apply to trainers and assessors. If you are proven to be negligent in an act, then you may have to compensate the injured party. This applies to individuals as well as to corporate responsibility. Trainers and assessors are, in principle, *in loco parentis* to their younger candidates. This means they need to offer a safe environment, while balancing the need to experiment and develop independence. If you and the organisation have taken all reasonable steps to ensure safety, yet a candidate is injured as a result of not following the rules, it is unlikely to be proven that you are in breach of the duty of care. So, if you are using equipment in a workshop, or scissors in a salon, or taking a group on a visit, you should assess the risk, warn of the safety implications and use protective equipment. All organisations including placements providing opportunities for candidates to learn skills and knowledge must hold relevant insurances and have a risk assessment for all activities. Failure to do so is negligence.

Diversity and assessment Equality is ensuring that candidates have fair and equal access to assessment. Although this does not mean treating all people the same, it does require assessors to design training and assessment around the individual needs of all candidates. **Diversity**, however, requires trainers and assessors to respect the difference between individuals.

The current diversity within the population of the United Kingdom is extremely broad. Embedding equality and diversity into all aspects of the programme is now seen as standard practice in helping to raise cultural awareness and prepare candidates for their future experiences in the world of work.

In addition, assessors need to be mindful of specialist needs of those for whom English is not the first language. **Bilingualism** and **multilingualism** is now common, with 16 per cent of primary and 12 per cent of secondary children speaking a first language other than English. This represents a 1 per cent increase on the previous year. Over 300 language categories are reported as spoken in the UK; this does not include dialects.

Annual School Census 2010. Department for Children, Schools and Families. http://www.cilt.org.uk/home/research_and_statistics/statistics/languages_in_the_population/annual_school_census.aspx (accessed March 2011)

Further, there is a promotion of the notion that:

> '... *bilingualism in a child or adult is an advantage and does not cause communication disorders'*.

The Royal College of Speech and Language Therapists (2006)

Assessors are, therefore, required to ensure that the language of the qualification or framework is accessible and comprehended by all.

Ethics in assessment

Confidentiality is required in all aspects of the role:

- In planning to ensure timely preparations.
- In appeals and disputes to ensure impartial outcomes.
- In feedback to ensure appropriateness of location and outcome.
- In evidence to ensure the security of information contained in personal journals, portfolios, or corporate information.
- In records to protect candidates' personal information, progress and assessment records.

The Freedom of Information Act 2000 gives candidates the right to access information that is being kept about them both on paper and electronically. The Data Protection Act 1998 requires organisations to store information securely and lawfully.

Finally, the assessor's attitudes, values and beliefs should never influence assessment practice or the way a candidate is treated (see also the various aspects of equality in Diversity in Assessment above). As a professional occupation a code of conduct is required of trainers and assessors.

The Institute for Education Business Excellence sets a code of practice for assessors. It requires assessors to:

- Evaluate objectively, be impartial, with no bias, declaring any conflicts of interests which may undermine their objectivity.
- Report honestly, ensuring that judgements are fair and reliable.
- Carry out their work with integrity, treating all those they meet with courtesy and sensitivity.
- Do all they can to minimise the stress on those involved in the assessment visit, taking account of their best interests and well-being.
- Maintain purposeful and productive dialogue with those being assessed, and communicate judgements clearly and frankly.
- Respect the confidentiality of information, particularly about individuals and their work.
- Attend assessment visits well prepared, having read pre-visit documentation.
- Dress in a professional manner and be punctual.

http://www.iebe.org.uk/index.php/code-of-conduct-for-assessors

Quality assurance and standardisation in assessment

While later chapters will cover these aspects in more detail, at this point you need to have a basic understanding of these terms.

Quality assurance is a process which ensures that assessment decisions are accurate and transparent. In order to provide clarity of this process you will find policies within the organisation to outline expectations and what to do if things go wrong. To meet an awarding organisation's guidance the following policies are expected:

- Assessment policy and/or procedure – outlines assessment procedure, guidance on special assessment requirements, strategy for QA, process for dealing with fails and referrals, and general guidance for teams.

- Assessment malpractice policy and/or procedure – guidance on how an organisation ensures consistency and integrity of assessment, including how the organisation will deal with cheating, plagiarism, collusion and falsifying records either by staff or candidates.

- Appeals policy and/or procedure – guidance on how the organisation will deal with complaints, disputes and appeals against assessment decisions.

Within every training and assessment provider, there will be people appointed to check the work of assessors. Again, terminology will vary here, but most commonly you will see the role of IQA. These people are tasked with the remit of quality assuring the assessment process. Each stage of assessment is subject to QA tactics. Those stages include planning, delivering, making judgements, providing feedback and record keeping.

For example:

- IQAs will call meetings to ensure that all assessors are working to the same set of principles. This is called 'standardisation'. Assessors may be tasked to review a piece of work and collectively agree the judgement; alternatively, they may be required to each bring in some examples and share these with colleagues – again to ensure consistency.

- IQAs will cross check a number of pieces of evidence to confirm that an accurate judgement had been made. The amount of evidence checked will depend upon the experience of the assessor.

- IQAs will co-observe assessments in the workplace to verify the observation process.

- IQAs will check records of assessment to check accuracy of completeness and check that signatures are bona fide. They will look at dates to ensure that candidates are registered in a timely manner, that evidence matches dates on recording documents and that assessment activities are carried out regularly.

These examples constitute the main aspects of the QA process in relation to validating assessment practice. Later chapters will explore this in more detail.

Disputes and appeals

There may be occasions when a candidate disputes the judgement made about the evidence presented by them. In Chapter 3 Quality assurance of assessment, you will find more detail about the process in the context of the role of the IQA. At this point assessors need to recognise that a candidate has the right of appeal against judgements. Appeals are likely to be either against the process – i.e. a candidate believes that part of the planning, delivery or feedback was unfair, or against the outcome – i.e. the candidate believes that the judgement should have been different to that recorded.

In either instance, the candidate should be allowed to discuss the disputed decision without fear of recrimination. During the candidate's induction, they will have been made aware of the process to follow in the case of a dispute or appeal. It would usually commence with an informal, verbal alert to a candidate's dissatisfaction. The assessor and the candidate would discuss the issue and, hopefully, either the candidate will understand more fully the rationale behind the outcome, or the assessor will review the evidence again and over-ride the original decision. Even though informal and resolved there should still be a record of the appeal.

An example of a record for informal appeals is shown opposite.

Irrespective of the potential outcome of the appeal, the IQA must be aware that an appeal is in progress. However, they should not request detail during the early stages in order to remain impartial should a

Candidate name	
Qualification	
Date of appeal	
Record of informal appeal	
Was the appeal/dispute logged verbally or in writing?	
Did a meeting occur to discuss the appeal/dispute?	

Date of meeting: ....
Persons present: Assessor:
                         Candidate:
                         Others (state)	

Outline the nature of the appeal or dispute?	
Was the appeal/dispute resolved?	
YES	What actions result from the meeting:
	Appeal lost: Candidate agreed with original decision following explanation, judgement stands.
	Appeal upheld: assessment decision amended in the light of review of evidence or policy.
	Implications for assessment practice: Complete and return this form to IQA.
NO	The assessor and the candidate failed to agree and wish to enter a formal appeal process. Candidate signature: Assessor signature:
	Complete and return this form to IQA.
	Date appeal/dispute forwarded to IQA.

formal stage be entered. An appeal or dispute conversation is a confidential discussion. If this is discussed with others before an outcome is agreed, then the candidate may have a justified complaint that the appeal was not held in a manner to minimise bias.

ACTIVITY 4

....

Collect a copy of your organisation's appeals and disputes policy and procedure and ensure you are familiar with its content. Prepare a briefing session about the process to use with candidates during induction.

Reflection, personal development and currency of practice

The role of the assessor is broad and the responsibilities great. Candidates rely on assessors' experience and expertise in their subject. To this end, assessors are required to continuously review their practice, refresh their skills and knowledge and offer their candidates a professional service.

Many awarding organisations and professional bodies specify the extent of that personal and professional development. Thirty hours per year of continuous professional development (**CPD**) is regularly advocated as a requirement to maintain licence to assess. While not regulated in the same way as teachers, trainers and tutors, assessors should aspire to this best practice model. The CPD is made up of:

- Professional updating: for example – by attending assessment updates, standardisation meetings, awarding organisations' training events or sessions to raise awareness of specialist skills in meeting candidates' needs.
- Subject updating: for example – keeping vocational skills current by working in the sector to update assessors on current industry or commercial practices.
- Personal updating: for example – improving own functional skills abilities, time management skills or personal development.

In summary, assessors are required to regularly reflect on their own skills and knowledge in order to improve their practice and offer an efficient service to their candidates and employers. Keeping of a CPD log while training is an ideal way of reflecting and learning from actions.

Glossary of terms

Assessment   the checking of learning and demonstrating competence

Bilingualism   speaking two languages

CADET©   Consistent, Accessible, Detailed, Earned, Transparent – the principles of assessment

Competence   knowledge of or ability to do something

Concept   an idea

CPD   Continuous Professional Development

Criterion (pl: criteria)   a standard of competence

Diversity – acknowledging that each individual is unique and recognising our individual differences in for example, culture, ability, gender, race, religion, wealth, sexual orientation, or any other group characteristic

Evidence   the output of an assessment activity; evidence of a learner's knowledge, understanding, skills or competence that can be used to make a judgement of their achievement against agreed standards/criteria

Formative assessment   interim or ongoing assessment

Goals   an aim or desired result

IV   Internal Verifier (old terminology)

IM   Internal Moderator (old terminology)

IQA   Internal Quality Assurer

Multilingualism   speaking many languages

National Occupational Standards (NOS) nationally set guidelines defining the level, size and subjects used in designing units of assessment

Ofqual Regulatory body, Office of the qualifications and examiners regulator

Pathway a route. Usually describing the combination of units to achieve the learner's goal

Principle a set of values or beliefs; a rule or moral code

Qualification a set of specifications (units of assessment) leading to an award, certificate or diploma of achievement

Quality assurance a system of review to confirm that processes are in place and applied to guarantee the quality of the service or product; systematic checks to provide confidence

Rules validity/relevance; reliability; authenticity; currency/recency; sufficiency; power of discrimination; objectivity (rules of assessment)

Standards an agreed level of competence

Summative assessment final or summary assessment

Units of assessment statements of knowledge and/or competence, clustered to make a qualification

Recommended reading

Ecclestone, K (1996) *How to assess the Vocational Curriculum*. London: Kogan Page quoted in Gray, D, Griffin, C and Nasta, T (2005) *Training to Teach in Further and Adult Education*. (2nd edn) Cheltenham: Stanley Thornes

Institute of Assessors and Verifiers – an organisation funded by member's subscriptions – to support assessors and QA staff and promote the sharing of best practice (http://www.ivalimited.co.uk)

Kolb, D (1984) *Experiential Learning: experience as a source of learning and development*. Englewood Cliffs, NJ: Prentice-Hall

LLUK (2006) *New overarching professional standards for teachers, tutors and trainers in the Lifelong Learning Sector.* November 2006, Lifelong Learning UK

The Royal College of Speech and Language Therapists (2006) Communicating Quality 3. *RCSLT's guidance on best practice in service organisation and provision.* London: The Royal College of Speech and Language Therapists

Wilson, L (2008) *Practical Teaching: a guide to PTLLS and CTLLS.* London: Cengage Learning

Wilson, L (2009) *Practical Teaching: a guide to PTLLS and DTLLS.* Andover: Cengage Learning

Useful online resources

Useful references for further reading about assessment are:

http://www.qcda.gov.uk/qualifications/60.aspx (accessed Sept 2010)

http://www.paa-uk.org/Qualifications/Regulated/Qualifications/QCF% 20Info/ QCF%20 Support%20Pack/Rules%20of%20Combination% 20in%20the% 20QCF.pdf (accessed March 2011)

http://www.cilt.org.uk/home/research_and_statistics/statistics/languages_in_the_population/annual_school_census.aspx (accessed March 2011)

www.homeoffice.gov.uk/crime/vetting-barring-scheme/ (accessed March 2011)

http://www.hse.gov.uk/risk/fivesteps.htm (accessed April 2011)

http://www.hse.gov.uk/pubns/indg36.pdf (accessed April 2011)

http://www.equalities.gov.uk/equality_act_2010.aspx

http://www.smarta.com/advice/legal/employment-law/the-equality-act- (october-1-2010)-need-to-know-for-small-businesses?gclid=CP7h7syP76c CFcoa4QodYhknaw

http://www.iebe.org.uk/index.php/code-of-conduct-for-assessors

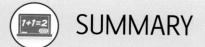

SUMMARY

In this chapter we set out to:

- Explain the functions of assessment in training, learning and development.
- Define the key concepts and principles of assessment.
- State the roles and responsibilities of the assessor.
- Summarise the main legislative factors.
- Outline the importance of QA, standardisation and appeals in assessment.
- Identify the relevance of reflection, personal development and currency of practice in assessment practice.

Your personal development

- You have reviewed the basics of assessment and confirmed your understanding of why assessment is important.
- In considering the language of assessment you have raised your awareness of the terminology and variants in current use undertaking further research on the topic by following links to relevant websites and reading.
- You have compared and contrasted the notion of formative and summative assessment and are aware of how to use these in promoting improvement and testing competence, while taking into account the importance of Kolb's Learning Cycle. You may have completed the activity to analyse and reflect on your own competence against one of the LLUK standards.
- You have explored the use of command words in setting assessment tasks and may have developed a dictionary for your candidates' use.
- You have investigated both the principles of assessment – CADET© – and the rules of assessment: validity, reliability, authenticity, currency, sufficiency, objectivity and the power to discriminate, with reasons why problems occur if the rules are not followed. In focusing on the principles of

assessment you have decided on the values you will advocate when carrying out assessments.

- You have examined the roles and responsibilities of the assessor and the link between that role and those of the candidate and QA.
- You have perused a list of legislation factors and ethics which should be considered when assessing candidates.
- You are able to briefly describe the function of QA and the ways that IQAs will review the assessor's work in order to guarantee accuracy and completeness.
- You are able to summarise the responsibilities of the assessor in dealing with disputes and appeals and are confident in knowing when to refer an appeal to the internal verifier.
- Finally, you have considered the importance of reflection and CPD in ensuring the currency of your own practice and compliance to professional requirements.

CHAPTER 2

Planning and delivering assessments

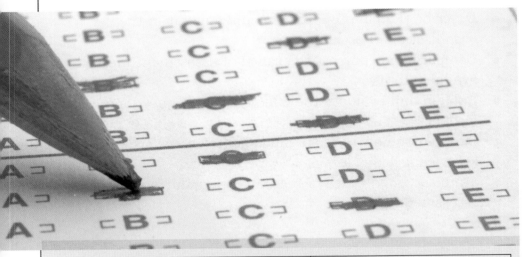

Unit of Assessment	Assessment Criteria
Understanding the principles and practices of assessment	2.1; 3.1; 3.2; 3.3; 3.4; 3.5; 4.1; 4.2; 4.3; 4.4; 5.1; 5.2; 7.1; 7.2; 8.2;
Assess occupational competence in the work environment	1.1; 1.2; 1.3; 1.4; 2.1; 2.2; 2.3; 2.4; 2.6; 3.1; 3.2;
Assess vocational skills, knowledge and understanding	1.1; 1.2; 1.3; 2.1; 2.2; 2.3; 2.4; 2.6; 3.1; 3.2
Understanding the principles and practices of internally assuring the quality of assessment	No direct references
Internally assure the quality of assessment	No direct references
Plan, allocate and monitor work in own area of responsibility	No direct references

LEARNING OUTCOMES

By the end of this chapter you will be able to:

....

- Describe the planning process and apply it in the organisation of assessments
- Compare and contrast the range of assessment methods available to use
- Explain and evaluate the effectiveness of questioning and feedback
- Summarise how to make judgements on performance and knowledge acquisition
- State the importance of record keeping during and after assessment.

Planning assessment

What is a plan? In short, it is a detailed breakdown (or formal contract) about how the candidate is going to achieve their desired assessment outcomes. It is one of the first stages in the assessment process, namely: plan – collect evidence – make a judgement – give **feedback** and review, and then you are back to the beginning and ready to repeat the process.

There are some protocols to observe when planning assessments:

- Ensure the assessment is fair (equality and diversity).
- Explain the process to the candidate – how, why, where, when, with whom, what?
- Link the plan to the assessment criteria – be transparent.
- Negotiate with the candidate and the employer and get agreement from all parties.

| Figure 2.1 | The assessment cycle |

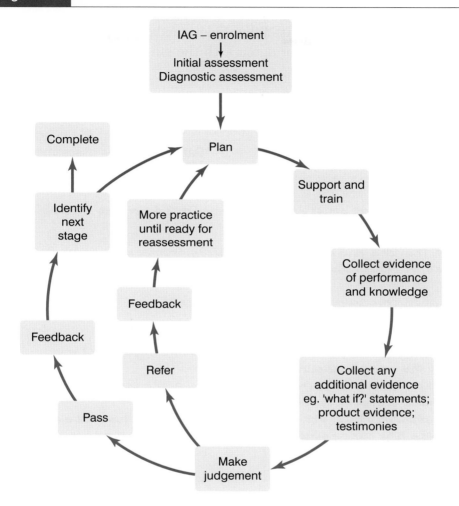

- Ensure that the planned assessment causes minimal disruption to the routine work of the employer's business.
- Confirm shift patterns and resources are available and suitable.
- Factor in any special assessment needs – to suit disability or difficulty.
- Plan to achieve success, not to fail – is the candidate ready for the assessment?
- Always prioritise naturally occurring performance over simulated or contrived performances.

- Maximise assessment opportunities – look for **holistic** assessments rather than unit driven.
- Ensure that the candidate fully understands the whole process and what to do if they do not agree with the outcome – i.e. the appeals process.

An assessment plan might look like this:

Summative assessment plan	
Name: A Candidate	Date of proposed assessment: 14th July 2011
Planned activity: To prepare short crust pastry and fruit for 24 portions of apple pie	
Expected outcomes/criteria/evidence (Units: Prepare and cook pastry products, Prepare and cook fruit dishes, Working safely and hygienically) Select and measure ingredients accurately Wear appropriate work wear and ppe Select equipment to prepare pie Demonstrate health and safety practices throughout activity Follow the recipe accurately Assemble prepared commodities for the apple pie, continue to assemble and cook dish for lunchtime customers Take photographs of product at various stages of the process Evaluate how successful you were in achieving the outcomes	
Evidence methods: Observation by assessor in the workplace Oral questions Photographs	
Plan signed/dated by assessor: A.N. Assessor 7th July 2011	Plan agreed, signed/dated by candidate: A Candidate 7th July 2011
Special considerations: Confirm with employer that menu is as agreed and products are available Prepare recipe card in large font Feedback after lunch to minimise disruption	
Feedback following assessment:	Actions for development:
Outcome: Pass ☐ Needs further training ☐	Assessor signature: Candidate signature: Date:

Planning assessments are key to a problem-free process. By observing the protocols in the bullet points above, you can ensure that planning is effective, comprehensive and meets the standards expected in assessment.

The what, why, when, how, where, who considerations

Most often used in questioning, the 'w' words are equally important in planning assessment.

> *I keep six honest serving men*
> *(They taught me all I knew);*
> *Their names are What and Why and When*
> *And How and Where and Who.*

Rudyard Kipling, Just So Stories 1902, The Elephant's Child

In your planning session, you will not go far wrong if you answer the questions:

- What: what will be assessed – you may need to write this both formally (using the units of competence) and in a way the candidate will understand (task related). The **goals** or short-term **targets** need to be **SMARTER**:

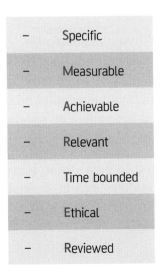

–	Specific
–	Measurable
–	Achievable
–	Relevant
–	Time bounded
–	Ethical
–	Reviewed

- Why: to achieve success in the chosen qualification, this maybe the long-term target.
- When: specify the date and time of the assessment.
- How: how will the assessment be carried out, by what method/s? The methods will be determined by the type of assessment: is it a practical assessment or is underpinning knowledge to be tested? Any **contingency plan** should be mentioned in case for any reason the assessment is interrupted.
- Where: specify the location of the assessment, e.g. in the workplace.
- Who (with whom): who will be involved, for example an assessor, a witness in the training environment? Is the assessor someone who works in the environment or a peripatetic assessor visiting from a training provider? Are there others in the workplace who may be affected by the assessment?

This detail is required to both create the contract and alleviate any misunderstandings. By being clear about the expectations (from all parties involved), the candidate will be more comfortable in the assessment situation. Irrespective of how much practice a candidate has, and how confident they are in their surroundings, very often the mere mention of the assessment word causes a shiver of trepidation.

In order to meet the 'HOW' statement, an assessor needs to be sensitive and aware of the characteristics of their candidates. 'HOW' is mainly concerned with the method of assessment, but some candidates require special assessment arrangements, which cause an amendment to a selected assessment strategy. Barriers to assessment or special assessment considerations come in many forms:

Using the acronym **DELTA©** (previously linked to barriers to learning in Wilson, 2009:51) the issues of access and barriers can be linked to assessment:

–	Disability
–	Emotional
–	Language
–	Technology
–	Ability

DISABILITY	EMOTIONAL	LANGUAGE	TECHNOLOGY	ABILITY
Chronic pain	Behaviour	Accent	Car breakdown	Absence
Dexterity	Child care	Basic skill needs	Computer skills	Inaccurate advice
Dyscalculia	Commitments	Communication	Fear of technology	Large classes
Dyslexia	Concentration	Cultural differences	Heating	Motivation
Hearing	Confidence	Foreign language	Lighting	Personal skills
Long illness	Dependants	Pace	Temperature	Punctuality
Mental health	Discipline	Rapport	Transport	Resources
Mobility	Employer pressure	Terminology		Short illness
Visual	Fear of unknown			Study support
	Finance			Support
	Hormones			Teaching styles
	New surroundings			
	Parental pressure			
	Peer pressure			
	Personal problems			
	Poverty			
	Previous experience			
	Returning to education			
	Stress/worry			

Types of assessment

Assessment is the term given to checking that learning has occurred and that the candidate is competent in the skills and knowledge of the occupational area. Assessment is not just something that will occur summatively, it will happen throughout the programme as a means of monitoring progress and is essential at the commencement of the programme to identify appropriate training and assessment strategies to meet your candidate's needs. Assessment also refers to the process of collecting proof of competence; this is frequently referred to as 'evidence'. This evidence is generated by undertaking an observation, questioning session, review of products, completion of assignments or another assessment method.

Assessment methods

There are several different ways of assessing or collecting evidence to demonstrate competence. The table on pages 45–50 describes the main ones that you will come across.

Quality versus quantity

Trying to collect sufficient evidence to meet the scope of the assessment criteria has long been a challenge for assessors. There is a tendency, particularly with inexperienced assessors, to collect too much, 'just in case' or, at the opposite end, not enough. This balance is something assessors must confront and test frequently. It is better to collect one piece of really useful evidence rather than a collection of things which only relate to parts of a candidate's qualification.

Here are some suggestions which may be useful:

- Read and comprehend the assessment criteria for the whole qualification, not just part of it. By doing this you will see where there is repetition and be able to attribute evidence to more than

Method	Description
Observation (Direct assessment)	Used in practical situations when a candidate demonstrates their competence (natural performance) while being observed by their assessor. This is considered one of the best forms of assessment – primary assessment – because there can be no doubts in the mind of the assessor that the candidate knows how to do something. The observation should be recorded either on film, electronically or on paper. A phone with a camera is quite useful, but ensure that you have relevant permissions before photographing or filming a candidate, especially if they or those around them are minors. Equally, employers might be quite sensitive to filming in their offices or on their shop floors. There may be occasions when the verifier needs to observe observational evidence to verify standards. Observation is very versatile in assessment as candidates are usually repeating their everyday activities and so will always perform at a level appropriate to their need and ability. Verbal questioning complements observation well.
Simulation	This is similar to observation, but uses a simulated activity rather than natural performance. The rules associated with observation (above) apply. While many qualifications do not generally support this type of evidence, there may be occasions when it is deemed appropriate, for example when using high cost materials or in dangerous situations. You would not expect an airline pilot to be assessed on his or her ability to crash land in a 'natural performance' scenario – this is best done under simulated conditions, which should mirror reality. Fire drills and first aid are other commonly simulated assessments. Assessors should always confirm the validity of using simulation as an assessment method by reading the Awarding Organisation's (AO) guidance on assessment.

▶

Method	Description
Project and assignment	These are usually a series of activities which collect together to make a project or assignment. For example, task one may be a written description of something, task two may be a presentation of some findings and task three may be a booklet or poster. Generally, a project is designed by the candidate and an assignment is designed by the assessor; both include a 'brief' which is related to the learning outcomes. AOs may preset assignments in order to standardise practice. There may be different assessment methods within an assignment or project depending on the tasks. The assessor will be assessing learning outcomes which relate to the proposed content of the assignment or project and are used during marking. Some qualifications also include levels of understanding, which are reflected in grading criteria. Assessors can differentiate outcomes of assignments and projects to suit candidate's needs.
Case study	Case studies are scenarios prepared by the assessor to test aspects of the qualification which are not able to be assessed directly. Alternatively case studies can be used to confirm that knowledge achieved in one situation can be applied in other situations. A case study will describe a specific scenario and have questions about the given situation.
Written questions	Essays: A discussion type of question which can be structured or unstructured. The assessor will need detailed assessment marking plans to ensure fairness, especially if the essay is around opinion and therefore has no right or wrong answer. The assessor should also consider what proportion of marks will be attributed to spelling and grammar, content, structure and argument, etc. To be considered fair, the assessment

Method	Description
	marking strategy should be shared with your candidates. Marking is quite complex. Marking could be **subjective**.
	Reports: A descriptive account generally used to explain a particular topic. Reports provide the opportunity to link theory and practice and offer chances for the candidate to cover 'what if' scenarios. There is rarely a right or wrong answer, so marking the report is best linked to the standards of competence or units of assessment to provide validity to the assessment. As they are written by the candidates the level is reflective of ability. Structured reports offer guidance on how much detail to include in the answer and can be helpful to candidates.
	Short answer questions: A series of questions where the answer is usually about a few sentences long. In some cases, e.g. the 'state four reasons for ...' type of questions, only a few words are required. Ideally questions start with how, why, what, etc. The marking plan should include all possible answers that could be offered by candidates to increase the **objectivity**. Short answer questions are quite easy to mark and are suitable for checking knowledge and understanding. They offer many opportunities to differentiate to meet candidate needs in that the complexity of the questioning is easily varied to suit ability. If completed independently, the assessor needs to check that it is the candidate's own work, maybe by asking a few oral questions or comparing the writing style with the candidate's usual style.
	Multiple choice questions (MCQs): A question with (usually) four possible answers. The candidate has to identify which of the offered answers is correct. As a candidate selects an

▶

Method	Description
	answer there is little opportunity to expand or probe understanding. They are very simple to mark; the AO may use computers to scan answer sheets and calculate the number of correct answers. They are quite difficult to write in the first instance but for the candidate they are relatively easy to undertake. This method does not support any differentiation of individual need, but is a very objective way of marking.
Verbal/oral questions (Direct assessment)	These are questions which try to establish depth of knowledge and are a useful assessment tool to complement observation in order to check understanding. For example – 'what would happen if …' type of questions. Verbal questioning is usually informal and sometimes unprepared in that the assessor sees something during an observation and wishes clarification or further information on a particular issue. Verbal questioning should be recorded on tape, electronically or on paper and the candidate should sign to confirm accuracy of answers recorded. Verbal questioning is a very versatile method of assessment and is so easily adjusted to meet individual's needs that it is considered a primary method of assessment.
Professional discussion	This is a semi-structured interview where the assessor and the candidate discuss an issue and the assessor prompts the candidate into answering questions related to subject outcomes. It is very often used to link workplace practice to standards of competence or units of assessment. The method is particularly suited to qualifications which require deeper understanding of a topic or candidates who prefer the autonomy of free expression in their own assessments. It is an effective tool because an experienced assessor will lead the conversation to ensure all aspects are covered. However, authenticity could be questioned – did

Method	Description
	the assessor lead in a way that would elicit only correct answers? Is it really the candidate's own words/actions?
Peer and self-assessment	As an informal strategy it is very common. Reading through a piece of work to ensure everything is covered before handing it in is a form of self-assessment. As a formal assessment strategy it can be used in the format of personal statements, journals, diaries or profiling. All of these assessments require the candidate to write down what they did or would do in a given situation; this is then linked to a set of standards or criteria. There may be a witness testimony to authenticate the validity of the statements. This assessment method requires a good level of self-criticism and personal awareness and may need to be 'taught' before embarking on as a reliable method of assessment. Peer assessment follows the same principles although the review is undertaken by a fellow candidate. Authenticity is the main risk associated with this method of assessment in that candidates may not be familiar with the units of competence or be as confident in deciding sufficiency.
Recognition of Prior Learning (RPL) (indirect assessment)	Also known as 'accreditation of prior learning, achievement or experience' APL or APA. A system of recognising the skills a candidate already has when they come into training. The process of claiming RPL requires a candidate to work either independently or with an assessor to match their previous skills or knowledge with the criteria contained in the qualification they wish to achieve. The assessment of RPL requires the assessor to validate the claim and ensure the authenticity of the evidence and confirm that the skills and knowledge are current. Testimonies, product evidence and skills test may form part of the claim. The complexity of gathering evidence

▶

Method	Description
	may be perceived as a barrier to using RPL as an assessment method.
Reviewing products or artefacts portfolios	Many assessments generate products which will form part of the assessment. Things such as printouts, letters, booklets, photographs and video clips are frequently submitted to prove a candidate has developed skills to the required standard. The use of mobile technology and e-portfolios provides a mechanism to produce a sustainable (i.e. paperless) portfolio.
Testimonials (indirect assessment)	The use of testimonials is important when the assessor needs to rely on others who have a closer contact with the candidate. Workplace supervisors are a valuable source of evidence to prove that a candidate consistently works to a prescribed standard. Testimonials should be written against the units of assessment. However, frequently workplace staff are less familiar with the criteria and therefore the assessor would be required to annotate the testimonial during the assessment process.
e-assessment or online tests	All or parts of qualifications can be achieved using learning technologies. Paper based examinations can be replaced by on-line tests which give instant results. Paper based portfolios are being replaced by e-portfolios which require all evidence to be stored in a more environmentally friendly manner. The evidence is stored electronically on either personal media storage devices or using a training organisation's servers. See Electronic and mobile learning and assessment technologies, page 55.

one aspect of the qualification – this is generally referred to as **cross referencing**.

- Consider linking the job to the qualification rather than the other way around. Many jobs completed by the candidate cover a range of UoA and therefore will be easier for the candidate to understand.

This is referred to as holistic assessment – where the assessor considers the bigger picture. An example of this would be a health and safety unit. It is possible to collect a range of evidence to confer competence in health and safety. However, every job a candidate does in their work environment will then enable them to demonstrate their application of health and safety, supported by some 'what if' questions to check understanding or contingency plans. This would reduce the amount of evidence required and embed it fully into every task completed.

Assessment conditions and environments

The environment in which assessment occurs is as important as the type of technique used. In some instances the technique used will directly impact on the environment and conditions.

- Observations need to occur where the task regularly takes place; after all it is frequently referred to as naturally occurring evidence. An assessor must neither help nor hinder the candidate who is being observed, nor must other colleagues.

- Simulations may occur under replicated or virtual conditions – but these should be as realistic as possible to ensure that the scenario mirrors the event.

- Verbal questions will often be executed in the same environment as the observation or simulation. However, an assessor needs to be mindful that workshops are often noisy or candidates might be distracted, so consideration of the appropriateness of the environment needs to be factored into the assessment plan.

- Written questions, especially those undertaken under examination conditions, need careful planning. An assessor must consider privacy, quiet, desk space, timing and allowable resources, then plan to accommodate the needs of the candidate, especially for those who might need additional support (extra time, signers, scribes, specialist resources, etc.). An assessor needs to establish how much help is allowed, before it would be considered inappropriate. Guidance on this should be taken from the AO, as permission is needed to change formal assessment arrangements.

- Projects and assignments are frequently completed in a more traditional learning environment. An assessor needs to establish to what extent research is a requirement and ensure that the candidate has access to journals, books or the internet.

ACTIVITY 1

Holistic assessment

Consider one of the following jobs frequently carried out in the workplace and, using the National Occupational Standards, create a grid (also know as a plan or matrix) which shows which parts of the qualification can be assessed while observing the task.

1. Hairdressing salon: shampooing a client's hair in preparation for a cut.
2. Construction site: laying a foundation course of bricks for a garden feature.
3. Garage: changing a tyre on a vehicle.
4. Office: typing a set of minutes from your supervisor's notes.
5. Veterinary surgery: preparing a rabbit for a non-surgical procedure.
6. Café: preparing a steak and kidney pie for a lunchtime meal.
7. Care home: helping an elderly patient to dress.
8. Nursery: supervising a play session with a group of three-year-olds.
9. Office: retrieving a document from a computer for your supervisor.
10. Reception desk: dealing with a delivery of office stationery.
11. Leisure centre: preparing an exercise plan for a guest.
12. Beauty salon: preparing a client for a neck and back massage.
13. Newspaper office: receiving an advert for this week's edition.
14. Farm: assisting the farmer with preparations for lambing.
15. Restaurant: serving wine at the table.

To start this activity you will need to break down your chosen task into its component parts. You should also consider additional skills such as customer service, health and safety, equality and diversity. You may wish to expand the case study to set the context.

For example, Restaurant: taking a customer's order.

Observable items: approaches to hygiene and safety, appearance, communication with customers and staff, knowledge of menu (food and drinks), how item is served, organised approach – table laid, crockery, accompaniments, dealing with problems or unexpected situations.

Each of these topics is contained in the Level 2 Diploma in Professional Food and Beverage Service, City and Guilds 7103-02, Qualification handbook, 500/7478/7.

Watch point

Always apply the rules of assessment to the chosen assessment method. Is the method a reliable way of providing valid evidence, authentic to the candidate, demonstrating current practice and will it provide enough (sufficient) evidence to meet the standards? (See also Chapter 1 The principles of assessment: functions and concepts.)

In helping you to compare, contrast and decide upon appropriate assessment methods for a given assessment, consider the following case study scenarios.

CASE STUDY

The candidate works in a hairdressing salon and the assessor is the senior stylist. They work together daily. Clients book into the salon for various services, usually regular clients but sometimes they are spontaneous. In addition, the candidate needs to demonstrate their understanding of how to respond to spontaneous bookings as opposed to regular clients? How does the assessor need to plan this assessment?

CASE STUDY

The candidate works in a vehicle repair station. Every day work is allocated to the candidate in the form of a job-card; he usually works with one of the mechanics, but is well able to do some tasks with minimal supervision. The assessor is from a local training provider and meets the candidate on their day release day and visits the garage monthly. The assessor always meets the garage supervisor when he visits. How should the assessor plan assessments for this candidate?

CASE STUDY

A candidate visits the training provider having returned to work following maternity leave. She is now a receptionist and is the first point of contact for employees and guests visiting the company. She worked in an office as an administrator prior to having a baby and is now considering an apprenticeship in customer services. How will you advise the candidate in presenting her previous experience towards her new qualification?

CASE STUDY

Students in the college have to attend sessions in the training restaurant as part of their hospitality and catering course. They have a rota which requires them to work in the kitchen, restaurant, reception desk and bar. In addition they have practical sessions in a skills kitchen. How can the college activities link to the assessments for their course? How would you explain the difference between activities undertaken in skills development, the training restaurant and their theory sessions? How can these contribute to a holistic method of assessment?

In summary, choosing assessment methods should always be linked to the candidate's needs and appropriateness of the environment.

Electronic and mobile learning and assessment technologies

Supporting assessment through electronic (e-technologies) and mobile (m-technologies) is becoming increasingly popular as the technology, equipment and access is improving. In an era of environmental sustainability the days of lever-arch files full of evidence is diminishing in favour of alternative storage strategies.

Online assessment has been a feature of many qualifications for a number of years. When assessment is undertaken through multiple-choice questioning many AOs host this through easy to access online testing software such as Global On-line Assessment (GOLA) or e-volve. Marking through the use of scanning software has been used for many years where multiple-choice questions or Likert scales are used to analyse answers.

http://psychology.about.com/od/lindex/g/likert-scale.htm

Many organisations now have Virtual Learning Environments (VLEs), for example Moodle or Blackboard. These are hosted through the internet or through an organisation's servers and intranets. They include access to resources, links to websites and documents, provide email facilities and support wikis, blogs and chat rooms. They complement, or offer an alternative to, managed learning environments and have the added benefit of being available 24/7. The VLEs can host forums on which candidates can have conversations, meetings or share ideas. These can be synchronous or asynchronous.

E-assessment is supported by recent developments in software and hardware resources. Digital cameras can easily provide still or video evidence of competence or products. Flip cams record activities and are easily uploaded (transferred) to computer storage systems. Similarly, the internet provides valuable links to downloadable material to support assessment activities. Voting systems provide interesting mechanisms to vary traditional questioning sessions. The increased access to WiFi and the development of smart phones and associated ppps is really broadening the scope of assessment and learning.

http://www.jiscinfonet.ac.uk/InfoKits/effective-use-of-VLEs/e-assessment

Assessors can accept electronic copy of assignments and other written pieces via e-mail and using 'review' in Word applications are able to provide a timely and trackable marking system. These and other electronic files used to collect evidence can be uploaded to e-portfolios using software systems such as Smart Assessor, Learning Assistant, Pass-Port, Pebble-Pad or iWebFolio.

Questioning techniques

Questioning refers to a process designed to find out what someone understands (or knows) about a topic.

Open, closed and leading questions Good questioning should be of an 'open' type, which means that the candidate has to think of the answer. A good question will test knowledge or understanding and contain opportunities to provide a full answer. **Closed questions**, have limited responses, for example, yes/no or true/false solutions – so a candidate could guess the answer. In **leading questions** the assessor includes a key word which might indicate a preferred response from the candidate – or even suggest the answer.

Nominated or directed questions In group situations, a nominated or directed style of questioning ensures that everyone contributes and that questions offered to candidates are pitched at the candidate's known ability. They are an effective means of differentiating or meeting candidates' needs. In a nominated style the assessor poses the question to the group, then pauses so that candidates can all create their own answer: the assessor then nominates (or directs) a candidate to give the answer. It can be made fun by offering play or pass options to minimise embarrassment if candidates do not know the answer. You may also try the 'ask a friend' strategy, in which a candidate can elicit

ACTIVITY 2

Following on from the descriptions of closed or leading questions, how would you re-write them to become open in style?

Closed question	Open question
Are there seven days in a week?	How many days are there in a week?
Is it correct that you inform your manager if you encounter an unexpected situation?	
Are you OK with that?	
Are you happy with the evidence in your portfolio?	
Do you know where your supervisor is?	
Leading question	Open question
I can see that you understand about PPE because you are wearing your boots. Do you understand about PPE?	What does PPE mean?
Is it true that blue and red mixed together make purple?	
How well do you get on with the people in the office?	
Have you improved your punctuality on site?	

the help of someone else in the group. In the worst questioning scenarios, the assessor leaves insufficient time for the candidate to answer and completes the question themselves.

Scaffolding questions Scaffolding questions are those that build on a candidate's existing knowledge or understanding. They enable the assessor to take forward the candidate and explore the extent of their knowledge and if they are able to apply it in other contexts or in problem solving.

Probing (or funnel) questions A technique which will take a broad topic and go into it in more detail thus digging for information. The assessor can use an **open question** to launch the discussion and then use probing questions to delve deeper into the subject. How or why did that happen? What would happen if ...? Can you give me more information about ...?

Effective feedback

Feedback is the conversation between the assessor and candidate. It aims to celebrate strengths, give constructive advice on weaknesses and identify areas for further development. It is essential in the assessment process; the main purpose being to let candidates know how well (or not) they are doing.

Feedback is the key to successful development of potential, increasing motivation and assessment. It is part of the learning process, because it tells the candidate how well they are doing. The quality of the feedback is as important as the quality of the teaching or training. Feedback should be frequent and meaningful. There are two types. The praise and criticism model is that which is based on personal judgements and is therefore subjective. In this model you list the strengths and the weaknesses. The constructive feedback model is preferred and more objective, because it is based on specifics and related to the assessment against standards or criteria. Constructive feedback can be positive, when good practice is praised. The assessor will appreciate and value what has been done and comment on how well it has been achieved. Constructive feedback can be negative, when improvement needs are discussed. Giving negative feedback does not mean giving the feedback in a negative (i.e. unsupportive) way. The assessor should not use sarcasm or anger. Be helpful – start with a positive statement and then comment on the improvements that are needed.

Watch point

Don't get over enthusiastic with the praise; it is far more effective when offered as a result of something achieved, rather than responding to everything as 'brill!'

You may also hear the expression feed-forward. Whereas feedback is based on a response to what has occurred, feed-forward is based on the notion of motivating a candidate to develop. It aims to address the difference between 'assessment OF learning' (feedback) and 'assessment FOR learning' (feed-forward). This might merely be an up-to-the-minute response to research in the field as effective feedback in its existing format has always been a method of aiding improvement, but it does reflect the fact that feedback tells someone how they have done and does not necessarily move them forward.

Feedback skills

Giving feedback is not easy; it is particularly difficult at the opposite ends of the feedback spectrum. If observed practice or an assessed piece is particularly good, it is difficult to identify development suggestions, or, conversely, it is difficult to feedback to candidates without destroying confidence when the required standards are not met. Giving effective feedback will test your own skills in listening, objectivity and explaining. It will improve the confidence of your candidates and develop their potential, but it takes time to get it right. Although you will be encouraged to give immediate feedback, in the early days you may wish to consider what you want to say before diving in – so give yourself a few minutes to think and plan what you are going to say.

Feedback should:

- Be planned and carefully thought about.
- Be delivered promptly after the assessment, preferably immediately, especially after observation or verbal questioning sessions.
- Be a two-way process – you can always ask the candidate to say how they think it went and get an idea of their understanding, checking their ideas for development.
- Be motivational – feedback increases confidence and self-esteem and therefore potential attainment.

- Be specific – feedback should only be about the assessment; it should be unbiased, without opinion, unnecessary digression or imposing your own standards.
- Offer choices and solutions – this develops potential.
- Only comment on things that can be changed – e.g. behaviours or values, not appearance or inner character.
- Be positive – use strategies that will encourage a candidate to develop.
- Be constructive – a balance of positive and negative comments should be offered on a one-to-one basis and as privately as possible.
- If circumstances mean that feedback cannot be immediate, then tell the candidate when it will be possible. For example: after the shift, when it quietens down a bit, when you get your next break, etc.

Constructive feedback is the title given to a form of feedback which is helpful and supportive. (It may also be known as feed-forward.) It is motivational in that it neither gives false descriptions of a candidate's ability nor does it destroy their self-esteem, but aims to develop and fine-tune skills. Whether produced verbally or in writing, this effective style of feedback follows a distinct pattern of:

- a positive opener
- a developmental statement
- a motivational close.

This is called the *feedback sandwich*.

By starting with a positive statement, you will reassure and relax the recipient of the feedback. Always identify something good, even if it is only the fact that they turned up on time! The comments you make should always link to the standards being assessed. The feedback should always be about the individual and you should never compare their performance with anyone else or anything other than the standards expected.

Developmental statements are the point at which you should make comments about things which need to be improved. It is good to get contributions from the recipient of the feedback. Using open questions will aid this process and together you will formulate your future plans.

Some questions you might wish to consider are:

- How do you think that the customer felt when you …?
- What would you do if …?
- What alternatives are there to …?
- Why did that happen?
- At what point in the process would you think about …?

If there is going to be a 'but' the person giving the feedback should build up confidence (i.e. discuss the positive aspects of the work) before delivering the shock. The use of the word 'but' should also be used cautiously. 'But' muddles what you are trying to say and confuses the message. 'It was OK, but …' *(Is it OK or not?)*

A contextual example of this is:

> *'It was alright but it wasn't very welcoming' is not particularly helpful. It seems to suggest a negative outcome. An alternative suggestion might be: 'I liked the way that you welcomed the customer and believe it would be improved if you'd stood to greet them.' This is of the same flavour but not as hard as a 'but' statement. In the second statement the 'but' is delivered as an 'and'. Therefore, is not as critical and more developmental.*

Ending the feedback in a motivational way will incite the candidate to take on board recommendations and leave them feeling positive about their performance, even if not ecstatic about the outcome. Ideally in a feedback session, you should try to get the recipient to identify their own way forward. This ownership of the actions needed to improve will result in a high level of motivation. It is at this point you can develop reflective skills in your candidates.

The typical feedback conversation example is:

- State what the standard is or what the assessment was about. Describe what has been observed or reviewed, without side tracking.

- Make a comment about what has been achieved.

- Offer alternatives like: have you considered ..., you could try ...

- Avoid 'BUT'.

- Summarise the key achievements.

- Make and state your judgement – you meet/don't meet the standards, you've passed or you need more practice.

In discussing feedback, it is worth noting the research of Prof. John Hattie of Auckland University (1999 and 2003). He investigated the effects of feedback on achievement and the ability of teachers to influence learning.

Having dissected the factors associated with teaching and learning and categorising them into responsibilities, he discovered, not surprisingly, that the teacher has a significant influence on learning. This furthered his earlier research which identified the extent to which feedback impacts on achievement. This all supports the current beliefs in assessment for learning rather than the assessment of learning. In summary, effective feedback is more effective in developing candidate progress than merely providing grades. This is generally because if a candidate is told 'that's a pass' or 'it's a grade B' they are more likely to accept that outcome without seeking development or improvement. When given feedback, 'most' candidates will attempt to develop future work. In combination they are able to meet both candidates' values and aspirations.

Additional reading on this research is widely available on the internet using Hattie, feedback and assessment as key words in a search engine.

Assessment decisions

Following an assessment and the resultant feedback, you will have to make a judgement. The decision will be a summary of what you saw that was good, the standard achieved, how much further development is needed. There will usually be parts of the assessment that are satisfactory, but there may be parts that were not so good – this may be reflected in the grade or pass mark. All criteria contained in the units of assessment must be met, which is why an assessment may consist of more than one method of assessment to cope with the things that don't naturally occur.

When making an assessment decision or judgement it is important that the assessor remains objective. The best way of doing that, to guarantee the reliability and fairness of your decision, is inherent in the make-up of the qualification and the rules of assessment.

- Always use the UoA specified in the assessment plan (validity).
- Always check that documentation is signed and can be attributed to the candidate (authenticity).
- Always check that documentation is dated and that the evidence reflects current industry standards (currency).
- Always check that there is enough evidence to cover all aspects of the targeted assessment criteria (sufficiency).
- Always apply the rules of assessment consistently without bias in all decision-making (reliability/fairness).

It is worth commenting here about authenticity and **plagiarism**. All evidence presented to confirm competence must do that. It must not be someone else's work. For example, in an office a candidate presents to you a number of letters that the candidate alleges to have composed and sent to customers. How do you know? You cannot assume that just because these letters were presented by the candidate that they were created by them.

Plagiarism is similar but refers to the passing off as someone else's published material as their own. It is more usually seen in written statements or assignments where articles, particularly from the internet, are included in a candidate's work without any citation or reference. Plagiarism breaches the Copyright, Designs and Patents Act 1988 in which it is against the law to reproduce material without acknowledging the owner. The acknowledgement is usually in the form of a reference citing the name of the author, the title of the product and the publisher. If using larger pieces of work then permissions from the owner need to be sought.

Unfortunately, one of the downsides of the internet is the apparent ease in which people can download information and cut and paste it into their work, or even acquire whole assignments.

How to spot plagiarism:

- different writing style or writing level to that seen in usual work
- variants in fonts and font size within text
- American spellings
- different referencing to that which has been taught
- typed work when handwritten is usual
- obscure references or sources of information
- different opinions/context to those made in class or recommended textbooks.

If you suspect something, you don't need fancy software tools to detect it, just type a whole sentence or just the key words, especially those that seem obscure, into a search engine and if it appears verbatim in the list of search findings then it has probably been plagiarised.

In terms of authenticity, it doesn't hurt to get candidates into the habit of signing and dating their work.

I confirm that this [assignment/essay etc.], is all my own work.

Signed: A Candidate.
Today's date

This does not stop plagiarism, but it enters the candidates into a contract concerning ethics.

Triangulation

There are various ways to achieve confidence in your assessment and thus promote effectiveness. One of the easiest is to triangulate judgements. This means, to use more than one assessment method to confirm competence. For example, a candidate presents product evidence; you check out understanding with some oral questions and seek testimony from a workplace supervisor. If the results of all of these assessment methods say the same thing then you can confirm competence. Each method is, therefore, contributing effectively to produce an assessment that is reliable and authentic and provides sufficient evidence on which to confirm competence.

Triangulation also provides variety. By testing learners in different ways, not only does it triangulate, providing confirmation that decisions are accurate and consistent, but it adds interest and meets different learning styles.

Depending upon the type of qualification, purpose of assessment and level of formality in the assessment, the decision will either be:

- Pass or fail – the assessment either meets or does not meet the standard required.
- A graded result – pass, merit [credit], distinction, which describes how well a candidate has achieved, but your feedback needs to explain the development between levels.
- Marks – out of 10, 20, 100 etc. usually expressed as a percentage.

The assessor should be quite clear in stating the outcome of the assessment. Saying the words 'you've passed' is very often the thing that is forgotten at the expense of creating good feedback. Also, sometimes the feedback is so positive that a candidate can misunderstand the outcome, maybe thinking that they have passed or achieved a higher grade than they actually have.

The 'F' word

The word *fail* is rarely used. This is because it is highly de-motivational. Rarely is everything so bad in an assessment that the assessor cannot comment positively on some aspect. If an assessment is not at the required standard, i.e. *fails*, you should consider alternative expressions such as 'needs further training' or 'not yet competent' or simply 'refer'.

Portfolios

Records are kept by candidates in the form of portfolios. Their portfolios will include records and evidence derived in their workplace and documents created by their assessor to record observations, testimonies and questioning.

What is a portfolio?

A portfolio is a collection of evidence – this is more likely to be the best or final copy rather than everything created during the training process. The portfolio tells the story of the candidate's journey from trainee to competence.

A portfolio of evidence, therefore, is a term used to describe the way in which the evidence required to demonstrate competence relating to a particular qualification is kept. A portfolio can be paper based, electronic (either through an e-portfolio or portable storage device) or a combination of both. Brown (1992) defines the term 'personal portfolio' as follows:

> '... a private collection of evidence which demonstrates the continuing acquisition of skills, knowledge, attitudes, understanding and achievement. It is both retrospective and prospective, as well as reflecting the current stage of the development of the individual ...'

While the portfolio belongs to the candidate, it is important that the assessor and quality assurer (verifier) also has access to it. The qualification assessor will need to see the evidence in order to make judgements about the validity, authenticity, currency and sufficiency of the contents. The qualification **internal quality assurer** (IQA) will need to see it to sample the decisions made by the assessor for accuracy and transparency. The AO will also require access, via an external quality assurer, to the information for sampling purposes.

A portfolio, despite the fact that it is an individual's record, does not need to include personal or learning materials as that part of the journey to competence is not assessed. It should be evidence relating to how competence is demonstrated against whichever qualification the candidate is registered. Collecting evidence in a logical manner will also enable the person collecting the evidence to reflect on their progress. So by keeping a list of contents, referenced to what the candidate is trying to achieve, both the assessor and the candidate will always know how much more needs to be done in order to complete the qualification. The principles will apply to any qualification for which a portfolio is used to store evidence. In the assessor or quality assurer qualification, you are additionally required to demonstrate your own occupational competence to be an assessor/quality assurer as this is a requirement of the role. Mindful of this, there is a suggestion in the format (below) that the candidate assessor or candidate quality assurer adds their CV and copies of relevant occupational certificates to their portfolio.

On the occasions when a portfolio is paper based, it is generally stored in a file or folder. However, it is not essential to copy absolutely everything. Whenever possible, a qualification assessor will view evidence in its normal location and 'testify' to its existence. This will ensure that folders do not become excessively large with lots of photocopies of documents. It also supports the notion that confidential material or records can be retained within the organisation. Similarly, products, for example, brick walls, cooked food items or clients' hairstyles cannot be 'put' into a folder. Admittedly, photographic evidence can be made, but qualification assessors observing or viewing the real thing are sufficient. This evidence may need to be seen as part of QA sampling, by both the qualification internal and external QA teams. This may mean site visits to view the evidence judged as competent by the qualification assessor.

ACTIVITY 3

Make a list of five typical pieces of evidence that could be retained in the workplace.

1.

2.

3.

4.

5.

(Answers might include: fire evacuation procedures, office procedures, cooked products from a catering outlet, staff appraisals, environmental/ layout of space, safe working practices, clients' treatments, confidential files, etc.)

City and Guilds, in these instances, recommend that when evidence is assessed in situ, the record of that assessment must state:

● Who and what was assessed and by whom.
● The date and location of the assessment.
● The assessment methods used to collect the evidence.
● The assessment decision.
● The units, learning outcomes and assessment criteria achieved.
● The location of the supporting evidence.

Qualification Handbook for Centres (February 2011, p11)

What constitutes evidence?

Evidence is defined as the output of an assessment activity; evidence of a learner's knowledge and understanding, skills or competence that can be used to make a judgement of their achievement against agreed standards/criteria. As such, evidence collected by assessors can be:

- Observation of performance
- Oral questions
- Written questions
- Products, documents, artefacts, photographs, video clips, records
- Professional discussion
- Personal statements or logs, reflective accounts
- Witness testimony
- Supplementary evidence – i.e. that which contextualises or explains the context of other pieces of evidence.

Each of these is discussed as an assessment method earlier in this chapter, pages 45–50.

Unfortunately, it is not possible for an assessor or candidate to just say 'I do that'. They need to be able to prove it.

An artist or model has used a portfolio for many years; it being a collection of pictures or images to prove their ability and versatility. A qualification portfolio is exactly the same; it is a collection of proof. Evidence may be stored in a file or folder (a portfolio) or electronically (e-portfolio or portable storage device).

Observation of performance Candidates may be observed by their assessors while working within their workplace. Observations will be planned in advance in order to ensure that candidates are prepared and their employer can expect additional people to be attending their establishment. Observation records would record the context and describe what has been seen.

Oral questions These will probably be asked following an observation. They will be asked to clarify something seen during the observation or to confirm something related to it. They will probably start 'what would you do if ...' or 'can you explain why ...'. Oral questions are not exclusively part of an observation; alternatively, candidates and assessors may select this method of testing knowledge evidence.

Written questions These are likely to be pre-set by the assessor and used to confirm your knowledge and understanding. Typically questions may be short answer type, written in such a way so that candidates can demonstrate understanding of aspects of the qualifications – especially those not observed or evidenced by producing products. They are unlikely to be tests or exams with time constraints – many will allow the use of texts to complete the questions (i.e. open book questions).

Products, documents, artefacts, photographs, video clips, records Work products are items, for example, business/service documents (minutes, print-outs, forms, procedures, diagrams), finished goods, commodities or commissions, or anything similar produced during normal work activities. Candidates should obtain authorisation to use any document or procedure. If using mobile technology to video an assessment or take photographs of others, candidates and assessors must ensure that appropriate permissions are sought and received before using them in evidence. This would demonstrate awareness of Safeguarding procedures and Data Protection requirements.

Professional discussion This is when a candidate and their assessor engage in conversation about a topic. In some parts of your qualification, it is not possible to cover all of the evidence requirements by observation. In these circumstances candidates and assessors will agree topics of conversation. This is likely to be a structured conversation and the assessor may ask specific questions or direct the discussion in a particular direction.

Personal statements or logs, reflective accounts These can be used as an alternative to professional discussion. Whereas a discussion involves a candidate and assessor, in statements a candidate writes how they do (or would do) something. A statement should be referenced to a particular topic rather than a rambling piece of text about general issues.

Witness testimony A witness is someone who is able to testify (validate) what they have seen. A witness might be an employer, customer or team member.

You will find these are the most commonly used methods of assessment. Candidates will produce evidence relating to performance – i.e. evidence of doing the job. This forms half of the evidence, the rest being derived from knowledge evidence – i.e. what is understood about the job.

Portfolio extras

You will need to check with your quality assurer whether or not there is a requirement to include the unit specifications in a candidate portfolio. Some assessors find it useful if their candidates' portfolios contain these to save them time when assessing. Other assessors provide grids which link the specifications to the evidence – called tracking sheets (see below).

Assessors need to mark according to professional standards, particularly relating to presentation of work, accuracy of spelling, grammar and the use of English. Assessors should always correct inaccuracies.

Confidentiality in assessment is part of the ethical responsibilities of an assessor and an IQA. An assessor/IQA is required to keep records securely, and respect the confidentiality of candidates and their employers. For example, an assessor will more than likely come into contact with systems and procedures in many different organisations. They must be mindful of 'commercial in confidence' which requires them to look at documents only for the purpose of assessment and not divulge information to others. If you use photographs in your portfolio, you must seek permission to use them. If people are in the photograph, especially minors or vulnerable adults, this should be in writing (from parents/guardians/carers of minors or vulnerable adults).

Copyright legislation exists to protect intellectual ownership and misuse of published materials. Plagiarism is when there is a lack of accurate referencing of published information. To overcome this, candidates should not 'cut and paste' or cite published works without referencing the source. For example, to cite a part of this paragraph the writer should write it as follows: Wilson (2012) states: 'Plagiarism … is a lack of accurate referencing of published information'. Then, in a bibliography or reference list at the end of the essay or statement, you would include the reference: Wilson, L (2012) *Practical Teaching: a teaching guide to assessment and assurance*. Andover: Cengage.

Supporting candidates to complete their portfolio is common. An assessor needs to decide at what point the support is complete and assessment starts. The evidence contained in a portfolio must be authentic – i.e. the candidate's own work, so it cannot include work which has been created by the assessor. There are ways of showing development within a portfolio, for example to include draft versions of evidence and final copy. This way, internal and external QA staff can see the candidate's journey to competence. In discussing authenticity, it should be noted that everything contained in a portfolio should be signed and dated. When assessing e-portfolios, signatures are not possible (in that e-signatures could be attached by anyone), so the assessor must make other investigations to ensure that the work is authentic and owned by the candidate.

Portfolios do have a shelf-life. Evidence contained in a portfolio is required to be current practice. This means that evidence contained in a portfolio which is more than 12–24 months old (depending on the sector) is likely to be considered too old to be valid. Awarding Organisations will provide advice on currency of evidence and it will change according to the sector. For example: the technology sector is advancing very quickly, so the evidence needs to reflect current versions of hardware and software. The Arts sector is likely to allow evidence built up over a longer period of time.

Exemplar portfolios are commonly requested by candidates. These are not advised because they remove the spontaneity of the evidence methodology. Candidates (and assessors) tend to replicate the style of the example and this restricts the efficiency of assessment.

Tracking evidence

Once all the evidence has been collected, it will need to be indexed and linked back to the assessment criteria of the award the candidate is hoping to achieve.

Depending upon the type of qualification being undertaken, one of the following would be an appropriate method to track evidence.

In these grids each piece of evidence is given a reference (or a page number) to indicate where it is located. Remember this could be at the workplace or saved to a file or folder on a portable storage device. Then the evidence is linked to the standards. In the first example you will notice that there is no piece of evidence that is recorded against 2.3. This means that any reviewer of this tracker would alert the

	REF	1.1	1.2	1.3	1.4	1.5	2.1	2.2	2.3	3.1	3.2	etc
Xyz document	p 5			✔	✔		✔	✔		✔	✔	
Observation 30/11/11	p 8	✔	✔	✔	✔	✔		✔				
Oral Question record 1	p12					✔	✔					
etc												

	REF	P1	P2	P3	P4	P5	P6	M1	M2	D1
Assignment 1	Doc 1	✔	✔	✔				✔		✔
Assignment 2	Doc 2				✔	✔	✔		✔	

candidate to gain some evidence to evidence it – alternatively it might be an error in the tracking.

> **Watch point**
>
> Assessors should always check the tracking sheets as they will need to sign to say that the evidence they have assessed does in fact cover the criteria claimed.

Tracking is a difficult task if a candidate is not very organised or the qualification has some complex cross referencing – so as an assessor you should be prepared to support them in this task.

Record keeping

Records are an essential part of the assessment process; they provide evidence of achievement and competence. They also have a wider purpose in respect of supporting organisational processes.

The part of the job associated with record keeping often seems bureaucratic and repetitive. It sometimes takes longer to prove you did the job than it took to do the job in the first place. These feelings are quite common and you should not feel guilty about having them, although to move on you need to see the value in the process so here goes ...

Paperwork: The necessary evil or the answer to your prayers?

The need to record assessments or in fact any other aspect of the role is essential to you, your candidates, your colleagues and your managers. Completing the necessary paperwork on time and distributing it to those who need it, is essential to support efficient and effective working practices.

Record keeping is best done in smaller chunks and not all left to the end of a programme; this ensures a distribution of the workload and timely completion of records which ultimately saves time. Records help you to remember what has occurred and act as a guide to others in case you are not available. A filing system suits methodical workers but not spontaneous types and so it is something that may need personal development time to fine tune. Records need to be kept in a logical sequence; chronological, alphabetical, by name, by programme or any combination of those. They may be stored as a paper record or saved electronically.

The stakeholder table: who needs records and why?

Who	Why
Candidates	• To provide records to evidence achievement, progress and support needs. Candidates will need advice on how to store their information.
Assessors	• To replicate progress records of candidates (in case of loss); to inform reports to others. • To inform reflective personal and professional practice. • To know who has done what and when. • To provide a record of the variety of assessment methods used. • To raise awareness of the overall assessment strategy of a candidate.
Colleagues	• To support team members during absence. • To share in team meetings and self-assess the effectiveness of their programmes.

▶

Who	Why
	Colleagues will need your records to be accessible and stored logically.
Managers	<ul><li>To monitor performance.</li><li>To plan for responsive provision.</li><li>To make strategic and financial decisions.</li></ul>
Quality unit	<ul><li>To generate comparative analysis across the organisation.</li><li>To compare performance with national averages and organisational trends.</li></ul>
Parents	<ul><li>To inform about the progress of their child on the programme.</li></ul> Candidates may not communicate well with their parents and so this is the only definite link. Don't rely on candidates to give reports to their parents, especially if they are anticipating less complimentary reports.
Schools	<ul><li>To create a link between vocational and academic studies.</li><li>To develop a standardised approach to a candidate's development.</li></ul>
Employers	<ul><li>To inform about the progress of their employee on the programme.</li><li>To inform their business processes.</li></ul> As the financial sponsor, they require accurate and reliable progress information.
AO	<ul><li>To register and certificate achievement.</li><li>To action and record external quality monitoring processes.</li><li>To inform responsive development.</li></ul>

Who	Why
Auditors	• To check funding claims are legitimate and business processes are legal and above question. • To scrutinise accountability and responsibility.
Inspectorate	• To quality assure performance at organisation level against national standards. • To justify appropriate use of public funds.

What are the consequences of failure to keep records?

- Candidate's progress is haphazard and unstructured.
- Mistakes and trends are not noticed so they continue to impact on practice, possibly in a downward spiral.
- There is a lack of accountability with no-one taking the lead on responsibility to candidates and other stakeholders.
- Candidates don't gain their qualifications, or if they learn the required elements they will not be accredited through a recognised organisation.
- Public confidence is reduced, which results in lower enrolments, which leads to fewer classes, fewer jobs, and eventually the demise of the organisation.

Hints and tips for record keeping:

- Keep copies for third parties.
- Write in an appropriate style for the reader – the candidate, parent, AO, etc.
- Keep notes about informal processes – development needs and actions, late work, resubmission dates, problems, etc.
- Documentation should give an overview rather than record every 'if, but and maybe'.

- Documents should be fit for purpose.
- Keep records relating to the process and product of assessment.
- Records may be self-devised or devised by the organisation – ask what is in use before going your own way.

Assessment documentation

Watch point

- Methods of recording assessments will differ according to the qualification type.
- Always use the forms agreed within the organisation.
- Suggestions for improvements should be made through the IQA.
- All forms should, at the very least, include the qualification title, names of the assessor and the candidate and the date.

The forms below are examples of format in order to recognise style. They should not be considered as 'approved' documents. The forms described, which are examples and not an exhaustive list, are:

- observation records
- records of questioning
- assignment front sheets
- tracking sheets.

Observation records

These forms are most commonly associated with the recording of observed evidence. The purpose of keeping documents relating to observation is to ensure that *what is seen is accurately matched to the assessment criteria*. Whether this is completed by the assessor or the candidate will depend on how confident the candidate is and how familiar with the criteria they are. In my experience it is usually the assessor's job! The observation record would be a piece of evidence to demonstrate what was seen, when and should be confirmed or 'witnessed' by the parties involved – usually in the form of signatures. The most common use of observation documents is to record workplace activities. They are usually descriptive and are written as a chronological record. For example:

2nd March 2011 – Reception area of Smith's Engineering, Sometown. At 09.15, Sheila greeted the customer in a polite manner, asking the purpose of their visit and who they wished to see. She then used the telephone to inform the Director's secretary that the visitor had arrived. Sheila gave the visitor's name and the company they represented. While waiting for the visitor to be collected, she issued a visitor's badge and asked the visitor to 'sign-in'. Two incoming calls were taken using the standard greeting and directed to the extension required. At 09.20, as the secretary still hadn't arrived to collect the visitor she invited them to take a seat in the waiting area. A package arrived and was signed for; rang to inform addressee of its arrival. She smiled when the visitor left reception with the secretary at 09.25.

When writing up observations, it is useful to have a copy of the assessment criteria to hand and to be mindful of everything that is occurring; this will enhance the holistic approach to assessment.

An observation record might look like the following.

Name of candidate:	Date:
Qualification:	Level:
Location of assessment:	

A description of the event or activity	Links to performance criteria

Assessor's signature:	Date:
Candidate's signature:	Date:

Records of questioning

These documents are more associated with verbal questioning rather than written questioning. Written questions automatically create a record, but verbal questions could just happen. The purpose of the document is to provide evidence of what question was asked and the answer given (whether right or wrong). This should then be linked to relevant criteria. Valid questions are those which are related to theory and underpin a practical activity.

For example, following the observation above, typical questions might be:

What would you do if the telephone extension had been busy?

What would you do if the addressee on the parcel had not been a member of staff?

Why is it important to use a standard greeting when answering a telephone?

If a visitor is very early for their appointment, what do you do?

At the end of the record of questioning, it is important that both the assessor and the candidate sign to say that the document is 'a true record of questions and their responses'.

A record of questioning might look like the first form opposite.

Assignment front sheets

The purpose of an assignment front sheet is to provide a standardised method of briefing candidates on components of the assignment. For example, it will list the tasks to be completed and target dates; it will identify any key/basic or functional skills that are derived from the assessment; it will state the criteria for gaining pass, merit or distinction grades; and usually provide a space for assessors to give feedback on the work. It is customary that the person who designs the tasks should submit the brief to the IQA for approval before launching it with their group. This ensures consistency within the organisation and a double check before issuing the assignment to candidates.

Record of Questioning

Name of candidate:	Date:
Qualification:	Level:
Unit/Assessment:	
Question	Response given by candidate/learner
Assessor's signature:	Date:
Candidate's signature:	Date:

An assignment front sheet might look like the following:

Assignment Front Sheet

Qualification title:	
Unit title and number:	
Launch date:	Submission date:
Task	Criteria reference Including links to Functional Skills
Feedback	
Grade achieved:	
Assessor signature:	Date:

Tracking sheets

These are the forms that record progress during a qualification. They may be used in a way that the assessor can plot achievement of tasks within an assignment, units or modules within a qualification or framework or completion of homework/class-work activities. It is usual to record the date the unit/task/activity is completed. Best practice models include the date commenced and who assessed the work, with a space to date and initial if the work is internally quality assured. A similar document can be used to plan internal quality assurance strategies – i.e. identify which part of the qualification and which candidates' work are to be sampled.

A tracking sheet might look like the following:

Qualification title:									
Name	Unit, task or activity								
	1	2	3	4	5	6	7	8	Etc.
Candidate A									
Candidate B									
Etc.									

To be effective and meaningful, you should devise a simple marking code to visualise the progress. For example:

- / means a candidate has started on the unit/module.
- X means they have completed the unit/module.
- Always add a date when completed, together with the assessor's initials.
- If verified the verifier could date and initial maybe in a different colour pen.

Reporting progress

Reporting progress (or tracking as it is commonly known) is part of the record keeping process. The keeping of records is about organisation, transparency and accountability, but recording progress is the part of the process concerned with sharing those records with others in order to initiate a development. This is the move discussed earlier: record keeping is associated with 'assessment OF learning', progress reporting is concerned with 'assessment FOR learning'. As we have already seen, the benefits to the candidate when the focus of assessment is changed from measurement to development impacts significantly on the candidate's achievement.

Why does progress need to be reported?

Progress needs to be reported, quite simply, because common sense (and current research) says it is the best way to develop potential. If the assessor tells the candidate how they are doing, they can engage in a discussion to move forward, rectify mistakes and build on their strengths. It is highly motivational for the candidate to be told how well they are progressing. Equally, with constructive feedback, it is valuable to know what isn't going so well, and, maybe through motivational interviewing, you will come up with strategies to overcome this.

The assessor will have to report progress to **stakeholders** (see The stakeholder table: who needs records and why? above). There are three stakeholders directly involved in the assessment process: the candidate; their parents or guardians if under 18; their employer if employed.

Parents are also interested to know how their child is performing in the classroom. It is increasingly important that the learning ethos is shared between home and the learning organisation. If additional work is being set to complete at home, it is good to know that parents are helping to ensure it is done.

Employers are interested because they have identified training needs in their employees and have contracted with learning organisations to realise those goals. They need to know that their employees are getting value for money and that they are attending and contributing to learning.

How and when is progress reported?

- One-to-one reviews – informally and formally at regular intervals throughout the programme.
- Feedback – after assessments and with all marked work.
- Reports – once or twice a year as a summary to parents or employers.
- Employer forums – to develop partnerships and collaborative activities.
- Parent's evening – to formalise candidate development – this is more common in the post-16 sector.

The timing of reporting is only a suggestion; it will be determined by cost and availability of resources and staff. It is hoped that informal chats will ensure that progress is summarised and reported frequently with more formal monitoring and stakeholder reporting targeted at specific periods throughout the training period.

Glossary of terms

Awarding organisation   a body approved by Ofqual to create and certificate qualifications (AO)

Closed questioning   limited response type of questions

Contingency plan   planning for the unexpected occurrence

Cross reference   linking evidence to more than one aspect of the qualification

DELTA ©   Disability, Emotional, Language, Technology, Ability.

Feedback   verbal or written comments about the assessment intended to bring about improvement

Goal   an aim or desired result

Holistic   the big picture; the whole qualification or curriculum

Internal Quality Assurance validating the integrity of the assessment

Leading questioning a question (with an indicated answer contained within the question)

Objectivity without bias

Open questioning question designed to elicit a detailed response

Plagiarism the passing off of someone else's work as your own without reference

SMARTER Specific, Measurable, Achievable, Relevant, Time-bounded, Ethical and Reviewed

Stakeholder a person, either directly or indirectly, associated or interested in the candidate or organisation

Subjectivity decisions influenced by other factors

Targets an objective or focused path towards an outcome

Recommended reading

City and Guilds (2009) *Level 2 Diploma in Professional Food and Beverage Service, 7103-02*, Qualification handbook, 500/7478/7. November 2009.

Fautley, M and Savage, J (2008) *Assessment for Learning and Teaching in Secondary Schools*. Exeter: Learning Matters

Gardener, J (ed) (2006) *Assessment and Learning*. London: Sage

Gravells, A (2009) *Principles and Practice of Assessment in the Lifelong Learning Sector*. Exeter: Learning Matters

Wilson, L (2008) *Practical Teaching: a guide to PTLLS and CTLLS*. London: Cengage Learning

Wilson, L (2009) *Practical Teaching: a guide to PTLLS and DTLLS*. Andover: Cengage Learning

Useful online resources

....

Balancing Assessment of and for learning. Enhancement Themes – various researchers summarised on: http://www.enhancementthemes.ac.uk/themes/IntegrativeAssessment/IABalancingFeedforwardAss.asp (accessed May 2011)

Likert Scales: http://psychology.about.com/od/lindex/g/likert-scale.htm (accessed May 2011)

E-assessment: http://www.jiscinfonet.ac.uk/InfoKits/effective-use-of-VLEs/e-assessment

SUMMARY

....

In this chapter we set out to:

- Describe the planning process and apply in the organisation of assessments.

- Compare and contrast the range of assessment methods available to use.

- Explain and evaluate the effectiveness of questioning and feedback.

- Summarise how to make judgements on performance and knowledge acquisition.

- State the importance of record keeping during and after assessment.

Your personal development

- You have looked at the planning process and studied its position within the assessment cycle. You are able to explain the protocols and design features of effective planning and have reviewed the factors which may provide barriers to successful assessment.

- You can describe and compare the various methods of assessment and have considered how they are appropriate within different assessment situations. By completing the case studies you have shown how you devise assessments to ensure that they meet the rules of assessment, i.e. validity, reliability, authenticity, currency and sufficiency. Further you have developed this concept by exploring how using holistic assessment minimises the quantity of evidence required to demonstrate competence.

- You have reviewed the importance of an appropriate environment in which to carry out your assessment.

- You have analysed how you can modify your questioning techniques to ensure that you are able to assess the knowledge and understanding of your candidates. You can differentiate questions by using different techniques for individual and group situations. You have practiced re-writing questions to make them more efficient in gathering accurate information.

- You explain the importance of effective feedback in both assessment of learning and assessment for learning. In each you can use feedback to express achievement and development of candidates' competence, following a constructive feedback model. You have scrutinised the protocols required in delivering an effective feedback session.

- You have evaluated the importance of making accurate judgements following an assessment. You are able to explain how to judge evidence against the rules of assessment.

- Finally, you have noted the importance of record keeping both in recording judgements and their part in reporting progress to stakeholders. You have looked at some examples of recording documents and are able to critically evaluate how they are fit for purpose.

CHAPTER 3

Quality assurance of assessment

Unit of Assessment	Assessment Criteria
Understanding the principles and practices of assessment	8.1; 8.3
Assess occupational competence in the work environment	4.1; 4.2
Assess vocational skills, knowledge and understanding	4.1; 4.2
Understanding the principles and practices of internally assuring the quality of assessment	1.1; 1.2; 1.3; 1.4; 4.2; 4.3; 5.1 6.1 Legislation: see Chapter 1 6.4 Equality and Diversity: see Chapter 1
Internally assure the quality of assessment	2.2; 2.3; 2.6; 3.1; 3.2; 4.1; 4.2; 5.1 Legislation: see Chapter 1 5.2 Equality and Diversity: see Chapter 1
Plan, allocate and monitor work in own area of responsibility	No direct links although underpins management of quality assurance

LEARNING OUTCOMES

By the end of this chapter you will be able to:

....

- Review the regulations and requirements of QA
- Explain the main functions and principles of QA models
- Define the key terms relating to QA
- State the roles and responsibilities of the QA practitioner
- Explain the disputes and appeals process
- Identify the key external organisations involved in the QA processes.

The regulations and requirements of quality assurance

In England, the Office of the Qualifications and Examinations Regulation (**Ofqual**) is bound under **statute** to ensure that **awarding organisations** and their approved centres comply with a set of **regulations** relating to **quality assurance**. They are also responsible for vocational qualifications in Northern Ireland. University degrees are regulated by the Quality Assurance Agency (QAA).

In respect of Ofqual, the regulations are:

- The Statutory Regulation of External Qualifications in England, Wales and Northern Ireland 2004
- NVQ Code of Practice 2006 (revised)
- Regulatory Principles for e-Assessment 2007
- Regulatory Arrangements for the Qualifications and Credit Framework 2008
- Operating rules for using the term 'NVQ' in a QCF qualification title 2008
- The Apprenticeship, Skills, Children and Learning Act 2009

You do not need to be able to recite these, but you should know that they underpin the values of delivering and assessing **accredited** qualifications. The various regulations aim to meet the needs of learners, maintain standards and comparability, promote public confidence, support equality and diversity and ensure value for money. To this end they specify that AOs and approved centres must:

- Maintain standards by confirming compliance to approval criteria.
- Offer a robust, consistent approach to QA and internal **verification**.
- **Sample** assessment decisions to confirm validity and authenticity.
- Provide valid and reliable outcomes against NOS.
- Keep accurate records relating to assessment decisions.
- Have policies and **procedures** in place for assessment and QA.
- Provide administrative systems to support **registration** and **certification**.
- Ensure that QA systems are consistently applied.
- Recruit appropriate staff to ensure integrity in all aspects of provision.
- State clear roles and responsibilities of staff to maintain high standards.
- Ensure staff have relevant qualifications and experience to undertake their roles.
- Review and evaluate to promote improvements.
- Have effective systems to recruit candidates and ensure their needs are met.
- Provide human and physical resources to support the delivery and assessment of accredited qualifications.
- Ensure fairness in assessment with appropriate references to appeals processes.

Ofqual also regulates vocational qualifications in Northern Ireland, with the Council for the Curriculum, Examinations and Assessment (CCEA) which regulates other qualifications in Northern Ireland.

In Scotland, qualifications are regulated by the Scottish Qualifications Authority (SQA).

In Wales, the regulatory body is the Department for Children, Education, Lifelong Learning and Skills (DCELLS).

In Eire, the National Qualifications Authority of Ireland (NQAI) has responsibility.

Useful online resources

For additional detailed information use the following links to the websites:
Ofqual: http://www.ofqual.gov.uk/
CCEA: http://www.rewardinglearning.org.uk/
SQA: http://www.sqa.org.uk/
DCELLS: http://wales.gov.uk/
NQAI: http://www.nqai.ie/

This chapter sets out to explore how this can be achieved.

Quality assurance models

Quality assurance is a business model which manages **quality control** systems to reassure senior managers and other stakeholders that systems are in place to guarantee the output of the organisation – in training terms the timely success of its candidates. Quality assurance systems will check that processes are fit for purpose, value for money, of a high standard and that they meet legal and regulatory requirements. Following the QA **process**, **quality improvement** is a mechanism to record the required and/or necessary developments and then monitor progress toward achievement of any identified goals. Quality improvement is informed by the outcomes of QA strategies. Quality assurance systems, therefore, are a continuous cycle of audit, review and development aimed to:

> *'Delight the customer by fully meeting their needs and expectations.'*

> http://www.businessballs.com

In all aspects of quality, the customer experience should be at the core, but it also has sound business principles. Quality assurance increases the levels of confidence in the value of assessment and the decisions made during assessment. It is a series of mechanisms or policies for ensuring reliable, effective assessment, i.e. guarantees of quality. Quality assurance also provides the mechanism to identify error and implement improvements. A wider purpose of QA is to assure the integrity of product nationally, to set entry and exit standards that are equal so that all stakeholders know that, regardless of where the qualification was achieved, the outcomes are equal. This is one of the main differences between accredited qualifications and un-accredited company training. Accredited qualifications have to be seen to be of a specific standard, whereas company training is designed to meet the unique requirements of a particular organisation – these un-accredited qualifications are not regulated by Ofqual. Both assure quality of provision, but company training certificates are less transferable between other sectors due to the training being designed around individual company practices.

In any QA model, the principle driver will be to strive for excellence. In a Total Quality Management (TQM) strategy, there is zero tolerance towards poor quality and a notion that quality is at the heart of an organisation rather than a process of the organisation. The TQM motto is 'right first time'. Total quality management focuses on the customer and advocates an 'everyone is committed to quality' strategy.

Standards model An organisation positions itself against a set of standards. The International Organization for Standardization (ISO) and business excellence models are examples of typical QA models which use standards to determine the quality of the product or organisation.

Benchmarking model An organisation pitches itself against others or sets of perceived good practice. This can be internal – one department against another, or with competitors, or looking at functions or general performance. This model is used by Ofsted.

Team ethos model The organisation measures itself according to values and contributions, particularly relating to staff. They look at these values and how they promote its services, through training and development and a collective strategy to strive for best practice. Investors in People is an example of this model.

Motivational leadership model In this model there is a notion of 'evolution not revelation'. This means that organisations look for small steps towards excellence and aim to be more reflective. Originating in Japan, *Kaizan* is Japanese for 'improvement' and forms the basis of many motivational theorists' works. These advocate that organisations that create ownership of the quality encourage a culture of continuous development.

In the context of assessment, quality systems provide a means for **intervention**. Quality is driven by effective leadership and works best in the absence of a blame culture. Staff at all levels need to commit to the same high standards and generally, if one aspect of the process goes wrong, very often the others will in something of chain reaction.

> # Quality = a better way of working.
> # Prevention is better than cure.

This statement means that effective quality systems, as well as checking compliance, need to be able to locate the cause of the problem, preferably before it occurs. Errors are minimised when procedures are followed.

The aspects of an organisation which will be subject to QA include:

- the learner experience
- training, assessment, verification and **moderation**
- support for candidates
- complaints, **appeals** and **disputes**
- self-assessment
- procedures and documentation.

 ACTIVITY 1

Take one aspect of your job role and investigate how it is quality assured. Consider how it is done and when it is done. Who is involved and how is it reported. Give an example of something that has improved as a result of a QA intervention.

One of the main methods of assuring quality is to have good policies and procedures which will guide staff on the expectations and protocols used within the organisation. You would expect to see the following:

- Assessment **policy** and/or procedure – outlines assessment procedure, guidance on special assessment requirements, strategy for QA, process for dealing with fails and referrals, and general guidance for teams.
- Assessment malpractice policy and/or procedure – guidance on how an organisation ensures consistency and integrity of assessment, including how the organisation will deal with cheating, plagiarism, collusion, or falsifying records either by staff or candidates.
- Appeals policy and/or procedure – guidance on how the organisation will deal with disputes and appeals against assessment decisions.
- Internal quality assurance (IQA) policy and/or procedure – outlines the procedures for ensuring accurate and consistent assessment decisions and processes to ensure that actions identified are carried out.
- IQA implementation strategy – a course or programme specific document to state how the IQA policy will be put into practice.
- External Quality Assurance policy and/or procedure – advises staff on processes to be followed in preparing for and after a visit from an AO.
- CPD Policy – outlines the commitment to training and development and how it is prioritised.

These policies would be supported by corporate policies covering the legislative requirements, for example: health and safety policy, single equality scheme and safeguarding. Additional policies relating to the recruitment, admissions and other aspects of the staff and learner journey will also apply to the QA processes.

ACTIVITY 2

Find the location and acquire copies of policies and procedures relating to your job role. To be sustainable you should ideally save these electronically to your personal storage folder on your computer.

Functions and principles of quality assurance

Centre approval

Approval is the process of seeking permission to run particular programmes, under the auspices of an AO. Thus, a training provider or college (or similar organisation) becomes an approved centre. Awarding organisations, who certificate the programmes, are required to meet stringent criteria (set by Ofqual) to ensure their QA practices are sound. Similarly an approved centre has to meet a number of criteria to ensure its suitability to offer qualifications on behalf of the AO.

Approved centres will receive QA reviews to ensure that they comply with the regulatory aspects of delivering qualifications. This is known as external quality assurance (verification). Whilst likely to be an annual event, the frequency is based on risk. An analysis of an organisation will determine not only frequency but the model. It could be a visit to the centre or a remote/desk based sampling.

Registration and certification

Every approved centre is required to maintain relevant administrative and management information systems to support the enrolment of candidates and claiming certificates. While organisations will vary, either the assessor or the IQA will be required to liaise with designated administrative or examinations staff to process registrations and certifications.

Watch point

Check the specific timeframes for registering and applying for certificates specified for your course or programme. The AO will specify timeframes for this in their assessment guidance.

Record keeping

An essential part of the process is that of keeping records to demonstrate that quality procedures have been carried out. In the next

ACTIVITY 3

Does your organisation or AO provide guidance on:

• The time between centre enrolment and AO registrations. For example: scheme registration to be completed within 12 weeks of commencement of the programme. Does the AO you use make any rule about this?

• The amount of learning that must take place before certification is allowed. For example: under QCF guidelines each qualification has a tariff referring to the amount of notional and guided learning – each credit in a QCF qualification attracts 10 hours of notional learning – of which some is direct contact (guided learning) and some will be self-directed study. Historically NVQs were subject to a 10-week rule in that certification should be greater than 10 weeks following the scheme registration. What is the notional learning for your course?

chapter you will find some suggestions for these. As an IQA you will need to keep forms relating to:

● How IQA is being planned to cover every aspect of the programme.

● Confirming that assessors are making accurate judgements. This may be by observing them making those decisions and/or sampling the evidence collected to inform the decision.

● The suitability of the staff on the programme. This will be achieved by keeping CVs or profiles demonstrating occupational competence and competence in assessment or QA. Specimen signatures will be stored on file to compare with signatures seen on the evidence.

● How the assessors are allocated to candidates. There may be certain assessors who can only assess specific units due to their expertise – a tracking sheet would show how that works.

● Confirmation that assignment or project briefs are approved as valid prior to their use by candidates.

● The amount of hours CPD and professional updating the staff delivering, assessing and Quality Assuring have completed.

All records will need to be kept for three years after the certificate has been issued. As this might mean an accumulation of paperwork, your organisation may require you to store records electronically or scan completed paper-based documents to store electronically. All records whether stored in filing cabinets or in computerised systems are subject to the specifications of the Data Protection Act 1998 and may be applicable to the openness of the Freedom of Information Act 2000.

The Data Protection Act 1998 states that personal data needs to be stored fairly and lawfully and only for the intended purpose (e.g. enrolment, registration, assessment or certification procedures). It must be accurate and kept up-to-date and not kept for any longer than is necessary. All data must be kept securely and systems must be in place to ensure that it remains confidential to the organisation. Individuals have the right to see information you store about them and question any decisions made about them.

The Freedom of Information Act 2000 gives individuals the right to request information, on a particular subject, from public sector organisations. It also allows individuals access to information stored about them.

One key document is the assessment record. This document summarises the assessment activity and provides a system to 'sign off' units as they are achieved. An example would look as follows:

Qualification title:			
Name of candidate			
Name of assessor			
Name of quality assurer			
Unit/module name	Date achieved	Assessor signature	Quality assurer signature and date (if sampled)

This could easily be modified to 'sign off' the component parts of a module or unit if required.

Standardisation

Standardisation relates to ensuring consistency and making agreements concerning the expected standards or content of an award. In a competency based framework this is checking the consistency and accuracy of decisions. In the context of technical certificates or assignment based qualifications, then standardisation will be used to create a consistency in marking.

Standardisation, therefore, is usually a series of meetings aimed at ensuring and monitoring the quality of assessment, the outcome of which is to provide a level of confidence in the assessment outcomes: credible assessment.

The Standardisation process can occur before assessment to set unified expectations and agree on how a particular part of the award is interpreted or to be evidenced. This is particularly useful when working with inexperienced assessors or new qualifications.

Standardisation after assessment is to agree the standard of assessment (or marking) and to check that there is a consistent approach to the validity and sufficiency of evidence. One of the pitfalls in leaving standardisation until the end of a unit is that if something untoward is discovered, the assessor may need to go back to candidates and ask for additional evidence. One way of resolving this is for assessors to be cautious in their feedback and use expressions like, 'subject to moderation'.

Ideally, therefore, standardisation needs to cover the span of the entire assessment period. The standardisation process is aimed at ensuring all assessment decisions are equal. It ensures that assessors are fully conversant with assessment requirements and consistently make the correct decisions. It is also effective in ensuring compliance to the assessment and QA procedures. Where non-compliance is detected the team can together resolve issues and develop practice.

A standardisation meeting would be convened by the IQA coordinator and everyone involved in the programme would discuss the assessment process, identify good practice and support new or weak assessors. The team would be able to devise a CPD plan to support their development.

Some examples of typical standardisation activities would be:

- Every assessor brings candidate work. For example, a 'competent' judgement and a 'not yet competent' judgement OR one 'refer' and one 'pass' standard piece of work (or merit and distinction if applicable). They justify to the group why they have assessed to that level.

- The assessors agree on what constitutes good practice in a particular activity which they then use during their observations of workplace practice.

- Assessors submit an unmarked/unassessed piece of work prior to the event, which is assessed by the IQA or moderator. Then at the meeting everyone assesses the same piece of work, the outcome being that everyone should reach the same assessment decision, mark or judgement. This is also known as 'blind marking'.

- Every assessor involved in a particular unit or module brings ideas or samples of product evidence or assignments, etc. to the meeting to establish the expected standard for that unit or module, which is then implemented by all assessors.

- A particular aspect is evaluated, for example, the use of **witness** testimony. This would provide the benchmark for future activity.

The IQA would run these meetings, which should be recorded. External quality assurers will need to see evidence of how the centre ensures consistency and accuracy in assessment.

Second (and third) marking refers to a process similar to standardisation, when one piece of work is independently marked by another person to (hopefully) get the same result. It is frequently applied to written work.

Another important role of standardisation is concerned with ensuring that the assessment decisions made within consortia organisations are consistent. Here, there is a great risk of inequality borne from the different cultures and methods of working within an organisation. Therefore, when working collectively, effective standardisation is of paramount importance.

ACTIVITY 4

Select a unit or part of a qualification and make a list of how it should be evidenced. Use this to check against a piece of work assessed by a colleague and one of your own. Do they match?

Internal quality assurance – verification and moderation

An internal quality assurance team aims to ensure that assessments are valid (relevant to what is being assessed), reliable (consistent standard) and sufficient (covers everything) to meet the requirements. The IQA checks, through standardisation and sampling processes, that assessment decisions are reliable and that judgements made by the assessment team are accurate.

In the organisation there will be a strategy for quality assuring its training, learning and assessment. While QA is the responsibility of everyone in the organisation, an IQA will take on the responsibility of checking and auditing to confirm the quality and consistency of assessment (and other related processes).

Internal quality assurance comprises two facets.

Moderation The confirmation that marks or grades are accurate. It is a procedure which involves sampling of completed or assessed work to arbitrate on the declared outcomes. This may be done by comparing a result with agreed models or standards to ensure equality of outcomes against others in the sample. Moderation 'evens out' the assessment outcomes and limits variance in interpretation of standards which may occur. Standardisation activities used in the moderation process can be before assessment (to set the standard) or after assessment to compare to the standard and correct marking if necessary. External moderation will take place through visits to approved centres or by posting samples to a nominated representative from the AO. Moderation is most common in assignment based or examined qualifications.

Verification The confirmation that the processes leading to assessment decision-making are compliant, accurate and complete. It is more common in vocational or competency based qualifications. Verification may also include aspects of moderation, but is mainly concerned with process. For example, is the range and type of assessment appropriate to the assessment opportunity, is the documentation complete, are the rules of assessment applied when making assessment decisions? Evidence is rarely re-assessed during the verification process. Verification should take place throughout the assessment cycle (Chapter 2 Planning and delivering assessments, Figure 2.12.1). In order to create transparency in verification, assessors should encourage candidates to reference (index) their evidence against the units of assessment.

Supporting assessors

Another of the roles of the IQA is that of advising and supporting assessors, in particular, new assessors. The types of support that would be implemented would commence with an **induction** programme for new staff. During an induction a new assessor would be issued with guidance on the organisation's systems and procedures, any corporate documentation and introduced to key personnel. If it hasn't already been completed, a **training needs analysis** (TNA) would be started to establish the extent and experience of the assessor, their expertise being matched to units or modules within the qualification. Sample signatures would be collected and stored for future authentication of evidence. New unqualified assessors would require additional support until they had completed their assessor's qualification. Until qualified all of their assessment judgements should be **countersigned** by an experience, qualified assessor. This countersigning process also applies to unqualified quality assurance staff.

Experienced assessors would require less support but should still be introduced to organisation-specific information – a CPD plan or mentoring is probably more appropriate for them.

Continuous professional development for assessors might include:

- How to complete centre documentation.
- The use of the organisation's software programs.
- Assessment or QA updates.
- Attendance at standardisation events.
- Familiarisation with new units or qualifications.
- Subject specific updating or professional/industrial secondments.

In addition to a CPD programme covering current requirements, an organisation may choose to offer development to prepare staff for the future, including succession planning, curriculum development, quality processes or supervisory roles.

Once established in the organisation, the assessor will make assessment decisions. At this point the support needs will be around interpreting criteria, advice of appropriate evidence sources and methods – especially if working with a team collecting evidence holistically. New assessors will need all of their assessment decisions to be countersigned until qualified – this includes observations, scrutiny of product evidence, questioning sessions and feedback meetings. This is quite an expensive quality assurance strategy, but is necessary to ensure the integrity of the qualification. Assessors should, therefore, gain their assessor (or IQA qualifications) promptly, even though many AOs will give them up to 18 months to achieve.

Following quality assurance sampling or standardisation any actions required must be clearly imparted to the assessor. In many cases the IQA and the assessor will sign the IQA sampling record to agree the actions and how/when they will be resolved. It is important that those records are re-visited when the actions are completed in order to 'close-the-loop'. Any corrective actions taken should be signed off to demonstrate successful completion of the actions. The corrective actions will either be:

Essential: i.e. must be completed to enable the candidate to progress.

Advisory: i.e. should be completed in future assessments to raise standards.

Desirable: i.e. could be completed to develop professional and occupation standards.

> ## Watch point
>
> Experienced assessors and QA staff who already hold an Assessor or QA qualification (D32, D33 or D34; A1, A2 or V2) do not need to re-qualify. However, they are required to maintain their professional practice and ensure that their practice complies with current NOS.

 ## ACTIVITY 5

Look at the following scenarios and decide what the recommended corrective actions should be and whether those actions should be considered essential, advisory or desirable.

Scenario	Recommended actions: Corrective action status:
The questioning record states the questions asked and the assessor has noted 'correctly answered' in the answer box.	
The assessment record has not been signed and dated by the candidate.	
The witness testimony from the candidate's employer is written very descriptively and does not comment on how well the candidate has completed the activity.	
It has been five years since the assessor worked in the occupational sector.	
One criterion about 'what to do in case of fire' has been evidenced with a copy of the evacuation procedure.	

Sampling

Internal quality assurance is carried out through a process of sampling assessments. Over the period of the qualification, the work of every assessor, every learner, at every location should be sampled. The amount of sampling will depend on the experience of the assessor, the age of the qualification and the number of learners. It is determined at organisation level and approved by the AO.

Verification/Moderation is on a risk basis. The following examples make suggestions about sampling size to demonstrate best practice:

- An experienced assessor using an established qualification with a reasonable caseload would have about 10 per cent of their work verified.
- An experienced assessor using a new qualification may increase the sample to 25–50 per cent.
- A new assessor with an established qualification might be around 70 per cent rising to 100 per cent for a new assessor with a new qualification.
- Unqualified assessors will be subject to 100 per cent sampling until qualified.

Some of the strategies used to quality assure decisions made by assessors include:

- Observing the assessor while carrying out a workplace observation.
- Observing the assessor giving feedback to a learner about an assessment.
- Interviewing assessors.
- Interviewing learners.
- Reviewing product evidence.
- Looking at records of assessment.
- Conducting an audit trail of dates.

Every organisation will have their own IQA policy, which will depend on resources. Quality Assurance should be part of the process of assessment rather than a product of assessment. This means quality assuring judgements as they occur; during the programme. Further information about how to plan and undertake sampling is detailed in Chapter 4.

Watch point

Beware the IQA who pays lip-service to the QA process. Look for detailed developmental feedback to assessors.

CASE STUDY

Assessor A has a cohort of 15 candidates working at one organisation in the outskirts of town. They are experienced, but this is the first time the assessor has worked with this new qualification since it moved over to the new QCF. One of the candidates submitted a week ahead of the rest and the IQA identified that the assessor had misinterpreted one of the criteria and the evidence provided by the candidate was insufficient to meet the evidence requirements. The IQA rejected the portfolio and told the assessor that more evidence was needed.

1. What strategies should the IQA adopt to resolve this situation?
2. What actions should the IQA recommend to ensure the error is not repeated in the remaining portfolios?
3. What preventative measures would have been needed to ensure this did not occur?
4. What are the implications had the IQA not seen the error?

Roles and responsibilities of IQA staff and other related roles

The duties of an IQA may include:

- Inducting new assessors.
- Confirming the suitability and competence of assessors.

- Supporting and advising assessors.
- Organising team meetings.
- Dealing with enquiries and queries about assessment, programmes and QA processes.
- Checking assessment processes both during and at the end of the programme.
- Monitoring records made by candidates and assessors.
- Tracking and monitoring the progress of candidates.
- Liaising with managers and other support departments to ensure compliance with procedures.
- Organising standardisation events.
- Dealing with appeals and disputes.
- Organise external verification visits.
- Communicating with internal and external parties to deliver an effective service.

In addition, they may need to:

- Recruit candidates.
- Organise inductions for candidates.
- Create administrative processes to ensure appropriate documentation is available and completed.
- Process registrations and applications for certificates.
- Train new assessors.

The basic duties of assessors and IQAs have been described here but you may find references to other roles and responsibilities.

 ACTIVITY 6

Research the information provided by the AO and/or SSC in relation to the expectations of the roles and responsibilities of assessors and quality assurers. Does your organisation have a job description for either role?

Expressions used to describe roles

Term	Also known as	Abbreviations
Awarding organisation – appoints the EQA	Awarding body	AO
External quality assurer – represents the awarding organisation to quality assure the QA processes	External verifier External moderator External examiner	EQA (EV, EM, EE)
Approved centre – appoints the IQA and assessment teams	Training provider College Work place	
Internal quality assurer – ensures the integrity of the assessment process	Internal verifier Internal moderator	IQA (IV, IM)
Independent assessor (second tier of assessment)		IA
Lead internal verifier or Lead quality assurer Co-ordinates a number of IQAs		LIV LQA
Assessor	See Chapter 1 The principles of assessment: functions and concepts for further guidance on role	
Trainer/tutor/teacher	Needs to be qualified with learning and development or teacher training qualifications	
Witness	Expert (familiar with the target qualification) Non-expert (unfamiliar with the target qualification)	

Lead internal verifier/lead quality assurer

In larger organisations/centres, there are likely to be programmes where there are a number of internal quality assurers. It would, therefore, be necessary to have an Internal Quality Assurer Co-ordinator (IQAC, IVC) or LIV. Although there may be a difference in their job title, their role is to co-ordinate the duties of a number of IQAs and be a first point of contact between the AO, EQA and centre staff. See Chapter 5 Managing the quality assurance process for more detail about this role.

Edexcel have recently created a role of LIV as part of a revised QA strategy. This role, for which applicants have to sit an assessment test called OSCA2 (online support for centre assessors), is where LIVs are assigned to an area of learning, for example Business, and all Edexcel qualifications within that sector are co-ordinated by this person. They liaise with Edexcel and are a key member of the QA team. Edexcel's external quality assurance staff are known as standards verifiers, who

sample work during the lead IVs three-year accreditation. In this model, the LIV is taking on the duties of an EQA in terms of checking and auditing verification processes.

Independent assessor

There is an increasing requirement to use IAs. This is to support the accuracy and **reliability** of assessment decisions. As many assessors are also involved in the delivery of training, it is difficult to assure objectivity when an assessor and learner have built up a successful learning and training rapport. By building another tier into the assessment, the quality of the assessment decisions are made more robust. Independent assessment usually means that a particular component must be assessed by someone not previously involved in the training, learning or assessment process. It is not validation of an assessment decision as this remains the role of the quality assurer or moderator.

Advantages:

- Assessors are protected from accusations of unreliability by using a third party to make certain assessment decisions.
- Learners are guaranteed unbiased judgements.

Disadvantages:

- Another tier of assessment means additional costs.

Witnesses

The testimony of others is invaluable to the assessment process. There are many events that occur randomly during the candidate's daily routine. If the assessor is not working in close proximity to the candidate, then these assessment opportunities would be missed. The solution to this is to use witness testimony.

As you would expect, keeping records about who is contributing to a candidate's achievement is paramount. There are two documents suggested.

The first collects sample signatures and the designations of those contributors:

Name	Position/role	Contact	Status	Sample signature
	For example: head of department, assessor, internal verifier, supervisor, colleague, witness	Please give a telephone or email contact – to be used to verify testimony	Qualified Assessor Qualified IQA Expert Witness – Unqualified assessor, but familiar with qualification requirements Unqualified assessor and unfamiliar with qualification	This should be the mark used when signing documents for a candidate/ learner. It might be a signature and/or initials
A TRAINEE	CANDIDATE	atrainee@ trgprovider.com	N/A	A Trainee
A Foreman	SUPERVISOR	aforeman@ trgprovider.com	Expert Witness	A Foreman

The second records the event being witnessed:

Witness testimony (also include detail about the candidate, dates, signatures, etc.)	
Detail:	Link to criteria
A Trainee uses the telephone more than 10 times per day to talk to our customers. They are always polite and answer the telephone with our standard greeting. A Trainee makes notes during the conversation and seeks to summarise key points regularly during the conversation. They close the call thanking them for their order or comment. A summary of the conversation is recorded neatly on the message pad and put in the supervisor's tray. If the conversation related to an order A Trainee completes the order on the computerised order system and sends it to the despatch office. This complies with our company policy.	1.3; 1.4. 3.6; 3.7; 7.6; 8.1

With regard to QA, a degree of caution will be necessary when using witness testimony as part of the assessment. The assessor must review the evidence to ensure that it complies with the rules of assessment:

Valid: Who linked it to the criteria – was it the expert witness, the assessor, the candidate or a non-expert witness?

Authentic: Was it signed. Can you be sure that the witness wrote it? Have you contacted the witness to check the authenticity?

Sufficiency: Does the text cover the criteria, meeting the evidence requirements fully? Are additional pieces of evidence required?

Current: Possibly the easiest, but does the text reflect current industry standards?

It would be unusual for a single piece of testimony to cover the requirements of a whole module or unit, but not impossible. The IQA should consider how much of the unit or module is suited to witness testimony – this would make a good standardisation topic. Expert witnesses are a valuable resource and it might be worth encouraging them to become workplace assessors.

External quality assurance and the tariff of sanctions

One of the quality assurance roles of the awarding organisation is to comment on the effectiveness of the IQA and to measure its confidence in the organisation accordingly. Organisations will strive for 'direct claims', which means that awarding organisations are confident that they are able to quality assure with integrity, and they are authorised to apply for registrations and certificates without constantly seeking approval from EQAs.

Every assessment team strives to get to a 'direct claim' status. This means that their systems and procedures are sound and that the AO has high levels of confidence in the assessment and QA strategies in existence. It is kudos for the team and ensures continuance of the organisation's good reputation.

During the EQA's visits to the centre, the EQA will ask to see policies and check that the associated procedures are being complied with. They will sample candidate work including those that have been sampled as part of the approved centre's QA process and those that were not sampled. They will make a judgement about the extent to which the centre and the team comply with the regulations. If it is discovered that there are breaches in compliance, i.e. there is a risk to the integrity of the qualification, then the EQA will apply a **sanction**.

The NVQ Code of Practice 2006 lists a tariff of sanctions which are applied when approved centres transgress from the regulations specified by Ofqual. While originally only applicable to NVQs, many AOs have adopted a similar series of tariffs to classify the reliability of the approved centre.

At the highest level of sanction the centre may be closed and risks losing reputation and the ability to deliver qualifications.

- Level 0 tariff: The qualification has **direct claims status** (DCS) without any identified action points.
- Level 1 tariff: The qualification has DCS with minor action points which must be addressed before the next visit.
- Level 2 tariff: The qualification has DCS withheld or removed. This is either as a result of a serious assessment or verification concern or a previously identified action not being met. The EQA has to sign off qualifications before a certification claim can be made.
- Level 3a tariff: Registration of new candidates is suspended. The EQA considers that the centre is at risk of not upholding quality standards if more registrations were to be allowed.
- Level 3b tariff: Registration and certification is suspended. There are significant serious concerns about the integrity of the assessment and internal QA within the programme.
- Level 4 tariff: Suspension of specified qualification. The AO considers that there is an irretrievable breakdown in the management and QA processes which compromise the integrity of

the qualification. The centre must note this on any future applications for course approval.

- Level 5 tariff: Suspension of all qualifications. The AO considers that there is an irretrievable breakdown in the management and QA processes which compromise the integrity of all qualifications run at the centre. The centre must note this on any future applications for course approval.

Appeals and disputes

REVISION

In Chapter 1 The principles of assessment: functions and concepts, you considered aspects of the appeals and disputes procedure as part of the assessment process and in the context of the assessor's role and responsibilities. You learned how to deal with an appeal in the initial stages. This part extends that process exploring the role of the IQA.

'Appeal' and 'dispute' broadly mean the same thing, however, they can be defined as:

- Appeal: A request to reconsider a judgement made.
- Dispute: A difference in opinion in an outcome.

There are two very important words associated with the process – fairness and consistency.

It is important to clearly express the process by which candidates can appeal against assessment decisions. This transparency is equally important to the candidate, assessor and organisation. The process should state the organisation's commitment to high standards of equality and be applied consistently throughout the organisation.

A policy will define what the organisation's viewpoint is. It ensures that its stakeholders are aware of its commitment to those who wish to appeal or dispute some aspect if its work.

> '... aims to ensure that all of its assessments and assessment results are fair, consistent and based on valid judgements. However, it recognises that there may be occasions when a centre or a candidate may wish to question a decision made.'
>
> City & Guilds – Enquiries and Appeals policy (August 2008)

A procedure will define the process a complainant will need to follow in order to make an appeal or log a dispute. It will define the circumstances within which an appeal or dispute is allowed, the time parameters (deadlines) and make assurances regarding confidentiality, impartiality and transparency.

While every organisation will have a variant on their policy and procedure, it should always default to the AO's guidance on appeals and disputes. In essence the process will follow a system similar to the following.

Stage one Candidate refers to the assessor to log an appeal or dispute. They will discuss, clarify and review the assessment and hopefully agree an outcome. Whether the appeal is upheld or lost, then the assessment team should review its assessment processes to identify training needs, support for staff, or confirm and rectify any resultant errors to ensure rigour is maintained. Where there is a failure to agree, then the next stage of the process is entered.

Stage two The candidate will formally state their grounds for appeal or dispute, usually within a specified timeframe to the IQA or designated person. The quality assurer will consider the appeal which may include a re-assessment of the evidence, another observation or interviews with all relevant parties. A decision will be made and notified to the complainant – again within a specified timeframe. If the appeal or dispute is still not resolved, then the next stage is entered.

Stage three This stage is broadly similar to the previous stage although the complainant is referred to the AO, who will allocate a representative to investigate the complaint; this is usually the centre's EQA. Their decision is final, although a candidate would have the right to appeal directly to the AO.

All stages of the process should be documented and stored securely in line with the organisation's policy. The AO will want to see records relating to appeals whether upheld or lost.

External audits and charter marks

As discussed earlier, there are many models of QA. In this section the role and purpose of the organisations involved in QA are summarised. Quality assurance will be undertaken by teams from within the organisation, but at times will also be subject to external audit.

For example:

- AOs
- Inspectorial organisations: Ofsted, QAA
- Charter Mark organisations: Investors in People, Matrix, Training Quality Standard, ISO.

Each of these organisations or charter marks (and there is a summary of each later in the chapter) will inspect or assess to a set of published standards and make judgements in the same way that the assessor would make a judgement about a candidate's competence. Colleges and training providers frequently undertake assessment against the various charter marks in order to market their provision and provide a level of credibility to the public.

Awarding organisations

These are the organisations responsible for devising and accrediting qualifications. They entrust that responsibility to centres who agree to uphold standards. The AO remains accountable for the integrity of the qualifications. They do this by reviewing centre performance to confirm the effectiveness of IQA, by sampling assessments, confirming staff competence and providing advice and support to centres.

Ofsted

The Office for Standards in Education is the government department tasked with the role of inspecting quality and standards in education and training organisations. It publishes its findings on its website and thus it creates the opportunity for stakeholders to review quality of provision prior to deciding which educational establishment to attend. It uses a 'common inspection aramework' (CIF) to set the performance standards. It makes a judgement about the 'overall effectiveness' and 'capacity to improve' through seeking answers to questions relating to outcomes for learners, quality of provision, and leadership and management. The questions in the CIF are answered in the organisation's self-assessment report (SAR), which demonstrates how high quality is achieved, sustained and improvements are ensured. (www.ofsted.gov.uk). The current process is applicable to inspections in a four-year period from September 2009.

Equivalent organisations:

Wales	Estyn (www.estyn.gov.uk)
Scotland	HM Inspectorate of Education (www.hmie.gov.uk) – inspection of schools
Northern Ireland	Department for Education (www.deni.gov.uk)

Quality Assurance Agency

Established in 1997, the organisation seeks to safeguard and help to improve the academic standards and quality of higher education (HE) in the United Kingdom. It is funded through subscriptions from universities and project work undertaken for funding bodies.

(source: www.qaa.ac.uk)

The review process is the integrated quality enhancement review – IQER – and is a two-stage process. The developmental engagement precedes the summative review over a, usually, 12-month period. Each stage commences with a self-evaluation and students can supply a student written submission to offer their views. The review team conducts an assessment relating to the management of the HE provision with the second stage resulting in a published report. It considers the extent to which a HE provider maintains academic standards, the quality of learning and its public information. The IQER process is currently under consultation to revise the methodology (2011).

Investors in People (IiP)

A set of standards designed to recognise and value the importance of people and their contributions to business improvement. It mirrors the teaching/training cycle in that the standards reflect the planning, implementation and evaluative stages of development. The standards seek to address the answers to the following questions and assessors gather evidence from both managers and employees.

Developing strategies to improve the performance of the organisation

1. A strategy for improving performance of the organisations is clearly defined and understood.
2. Learning and development is planned to achieve the organisation's objectives.
3. Strategies for managing people are designed to promote equality of opportunity in the development of the organisation's people.
4. The capabilities managers need to lead, manage and develop people effectively are clearly defined and understood.

Taking action to improve the performance of the organisation

5. Managers are effective in leading, managing and developing people.
6. People's contribution to the organisation is recognised and valued.
7. People are encouraged to take ownership and responsibility by being involved in decision-making.
8. People learn and develop effectively.

Evaluating the impact on the performance of the organisation

9. Investment in people improves the performance of the organisation.

10. Improvements are continually made to the way people are managed and developed.

(source: http://www.investorsinpeople.co.uk)

International Organisation for Standardisation

The ISO is recognised throughout the world, and due to language differences has adopted ISO as its acronym. Based on the training cycle, it enables organisations to work more efficiently and effectively by checking that the systems and procedures are implemented consistently throughout the organisation. There are over 17 000 different standards covering a wide variety of sectors, disciplines and initiatives. The two most commonly seen in the lifelong learning sector are those associated with quality management and environmental management. The current series for quality is the ISO 9001 standard and the ISO14001 is the standard for environmental management. These international standards certify the process rather than the product.

(source: http://www.iso.org)

Matrix assessment

Matrix standards are service standards relating to information, advice and guidance. They look at the work of those involved in giving assistance to learners as they embark on their post-compulsory learning. There are eight standards:

Delivering the service:	Awareness
	Defining the service
	Access to information
	Support in exploring options

Managing the service:	Planning and maintaining the service Staff competence and support Feedback from customers Quality improvement through evaluation

(Source: http://www.matrixstandard.com)

Training Quality Standard (TQS)

NOTE: 19 April 2011. The Department for Business, Innovation and Skills took the decision to withdraw funding for TQS and is winding down accreditation. This will have the effect of making existing accreditations valueless as a charter mark; however it would still act as a measure of an organisation's responsiveness to their employers, pending alternative solutions.

This charter mark helped to measure how effective a training provider is at delivering their employers' needs. When engaging in a training programme the employer would have specific business needs and expected impacts of that training – for example: increased productivity, fewer accidents, faster response times, etc. For the employer, TQS is useful in measuring the effect of training; providing a benchmark for training standards; and how it impacts on procurement decisions. For the training provider, TQS is useful in measuring systems and the effectiveness of the employer/provider communications. It provides a statement about efficiency and therefore is a marketing tool.

Assessment is in two parts: Part A is about responsiveness to employer needs, Part B is about specific sector expertise, i.e. high standards of delivery in a particular occupation.

While inspections by Ofsted and the QAA are done to an organisation, IiP, ISO, Matrix and TQS are voluntary assessments selected by the organisation as part of its assumed role and character.

(source: http://www.trainingqualitystandard.co.uk)

A potential alternative to TQS is investors in excellence (IiE). It aims to deliver sustainable improvements within an organisation. The Standard is based on the European Foundation for Quality Management model (EFQM), which is widely adopted in Europe.

In summary, QA in assessment is a model that can be applied internally and externally, with the sole purpose of making guarantees about the accuracy of assessment. In the next chapter we consider the practical approaches to QA.

Glossary of terms

Accredited   a qualification written under Ofqual regulations

Appeal   a request to reconsider a judgement made

Awarding organisation   a body approved by Ofqual to create and certificate qualifications (AO)

Certification   a process of claiming a certificate following successful completion of a qualification

Continuous professional development   on-the-job training for staff (CPD)

Countersign   a guarantee of reliability in assessment decisions, made by unqualified assessors

Direct claims status   a high level of confidence from an AO, resulting in the ability to claim certification without a visit from an EQA (DCS)

Dispute   a difference in opinion of an outcome

Induction   an introduction to a programme or duty

Intervention   to interrupt for the purpose of resolving issues

Moderation   the confirmation that marks or grades are accurate

Ofqual   regulatory body, office of the qualifications and examinations regulation

Policy   a statement of proposed actions

Procedure   a way of working

Process   a series of actions to meet a specific outcome

Quality assurance a system of review to confirm that processes are in place and applied to guarantee the quality of the service or product; systematic checks to provide confidence

Quality control checks on the integrity of the process

Quality improvement process to improve reliability of quality assurance systems

Registration an official list of entrants to a qualification

Regulation a rule or directive made by an official organisation

Reliability strategy to ensure that assessment decisions are consistent

Sample a representative of the whole to show trends

Sanction a penalty for disobeying the rules

Standardisation process to confirm decisions and create norms

Statute a written law passed by a legislative body

Training needs analysis identification of required training (TNA)

Verification the confirmation that the processes leading to assessment decision-making are compliant, accurate and complete

Witness a person, other than assessor, who provides evidence of competence.

Recommended reading

Wilson, L (2008) *Practical Teaching: a guide to PTLLS and CTLLS.* London: Cengage Learning

Wilson, L (2009) *Practical Teaching: a guide to PTLLS and DTLLS.* Andover: Cengage Learning

Useful online resources

Useful references for further reading about assessment are:

http://www.businessballs.com/dtiresources/total_quality_management_TQM.pdf

http://www.ofqual.gov.uk/files/Regulatory_arrangements_QCF_August08.pdf

http://www.ofqual.gov.uk/files/qca-06-2888_nvq_code_of_practice_r06.pdf

http://www.matrixstandard.com

http://www.trainingqualitystandard.co.uk

http://www.iso.org

http://www.investorsinpeople.co.uk

www.qaa.ac.uk

www.deni.gov.uk

www.hmie.gov.uk

www.estyn.gov.uk

www.ofsted.gov.uk

SUMMARY

In this chapter we set out to:

- Review the regulations and requirements of QA.
- Explain the main functions and principles of QA models.
- Define the key terms relating to QA.
- State the roles and responsibilities of the QA practitioner.
- Explain the disputes and appeals process.
- Identify the key external organisations involved in the QA processes.

Your personal development

- You have reviewed the main regulations which apply to QA, considering both the requirements for AOs and those for approved centres. You are able to describe the role of Ofqual in regulating processes.

- You have looked at quality as a business model and are able to define the benefits of systems and procedures in maintaining and raising standards. You have considered a zero tolerance model and are able to broadly describe TQM.

- You have explored in detail the various functions and principles of a QA system. You have thought about the purpose of centre approvals and the link between the centre and the AO in processing registrations and certifications. In completing this review you have considered the records that you will be required to keep in order to demonstrate compliance to the regulations and comply with the Data Protection Act 1998 and the Freedom of Information Act 2000.

- You have focused on the functions relating to standardisation of evidence and can describe several different types of activity that would be deemed appropriate as standardisation mechanisms.

- You have scrutinised internal quality assurance and the role of supporting assessors and the checking of the accuracy of assessments. You have completed an activity which confirms your ability to compare the difference between the levels of corrective actions and how to make recommendations for improvement. Further, you have looked at the types of sampling systems available and how they confirm accuracy of assessment. In the completion of a case study you have demonstrated how you use information gained during sampling in order to improve performance.

- Finally, in this section, you have reviewed the levels of sanction that would be imposed should a centre be in default of the regulations.

- Then, you looked at the role of the IQA and their relationship to others in the QA stage and considered the importance of the role in bringing about high levels of confidence in assessment. When reviewing the role of witnesses, you have studied two exemplar documents on which to record testimony.

- You have examined the various stages of the appeals and disputes process and can define who is involved and at what stage. You are aware of the role of the awarding organisation as the final arbiter.

- Finally, in this chapter you have reflected on the roles of the various inspectorial and charter mark organisations and how they help organisations to develop and measure themselves against standards and position themselves in the public eye.

In the next chapter we will consider the practicalities of the role.

CHAPTER 4
Internally assuring the quality of assessment

Unit of Assessment	Assessment Criteria
Understanding the principles and practices of assessment	No direct references
Assess occupational competence in the work environment	No direct references
Assess vocational skills, knowledge and understanding	No direct references
Understanding the principles and practices of internally assuring the quality of assessment	2.1; 2.2; 2.3; 3.1; 3.2; 4.1; 6.2; 6.3 6.1 Legislation: see Chapter 16.4 Equality and Diversity: see Chapter 1
Internally assure the quality of assessment	1.1; 1.2; 2.1; 2.2; 2.3; 2.4; 2.5; 2.6; 5.3; 5.4
Plan, allocate and monitor work in own area of responsibility	No direct references although content underpins management aspects of the award

LEARNING OUTCOMES

By the end of this chapter you will be able to:

....

- Describe the importance and key attributes of planning processes in assuring quality
- Summarise the main sampling strategies
- Identify activities which contribute to quality assurance procedures
- Outline the role feedback has in developing assessment practice
- Reflect on current practice and plan to develop skills and knowledge

Internal quality assurance

REVISION

In Chapter 1 The principles of assessment: functions and concepts and Chapter 2 Planning and delivering assessments you have learned about the main principles of assessment and the importance of the rules of assessment, i.e. the assessed work is **valid**, **authentic**, has **currency** and is **sufficient**. You have reviewed a number of assessment methods and discovered the importance of planning, delivering, making judgements and providing feedback to candidates. In Chapter 3 Quality assurance of assessment you looked at the regulatory **requirements** of QA and explored the purpose of sampling and standardisation. In this chapter we put all of that together in a practical look at QA in action by reconsidering these components in the context of planning and delivering QA.

Any training organisation approved to deliver qualifications on behalf of an AO must have effective QA systems in place to ensure that the delivery and assessment of qualifications is of a high standard. These

Figure 4.1	The quality cycle

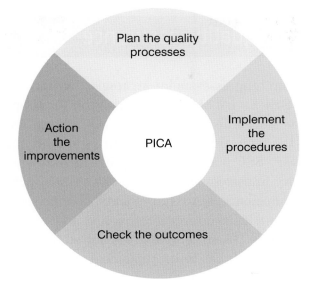

approved centres are responsible for internal quality assurance while the AO will undertake external quality assurance. The AO, during either site visits or remote activity, will check the policies and procedures of approved centres and confirm that staff comply with procedure and are able to manage the assessment and QA processes.

The quality process follows a cyclical strategy of planning, implementing, checking and actioning improvement. This is shown in Figure 4.1.

P	Plan for quality processes
I	Implement the quality procedures
C	Check the outcomes
A	Act on the improvements required

PICA is an acronym designed to help you remember the various stages of the quality cycle. Each relates to a particular aspect of QA procedures and on completion of the cycle there will be an inevitable requirement to recommence the cycle, thus ensuring continuous improvement.

Planning for quality assurance

The various overarching assessment strategies, written by the Sector Skills Councils (**SSC**) (visit the UK Commission for Employment and Skills website for more information on the SSCs http://www.ukces.org. uk), will define the main protocols for assuring quality for the qualification. Every SSC is required to define its assessment strategy to ensure integrity in assessment. It will cover rules such as assessor experience and competence, QA requirements, specific sector idiosyncrasies and guidance on interpreting and assessing the occupational standards. Then, centres are required to develop a working strategy and a plan which has to be implemented by all those undertaking assessment and internal quality assurance roles. This plan must also meet the requirements of the approved centre and the AO.

Those requirements can be broadly categorised as assessment strategy, legislation and organisation specific methods of working:

- Assessment strategy will define who can assess and the IQA decides what to assess, e.g. the frequency and issues such as the policy on simulated assessment.
- Legislation will cover the requirements of, for example, the Health and Safety at Work etc Act 1974, the Equality Act 2010 and the Data Protection Act 1998.
- Working methods will consider security aspects, shift working, acceptable dress codes, contractual or staffing issues.

In summary, the requirements of the AO and the centre cover aspects which will ensure that the assessment and the internal quality

ACTIVITY 1

Locate your organisation's assessment and QA policy and procedure and develop a strategy to monitor the QA of two assessors in your team. Be careful to include a sampling plan relevant to their experience and contingencies to address difficulty in interpreting assessment criteria.

assurance of the qualification is managed with integrity; is open, transparent and available to all; is executed professionally and is accurately and consistently recorded.

Watch point

This is not an issue of trust; it is a method of securing **evidence** to confirm that QA is testing authenticity, currency, validity and sufficiency. Quality Assurance staff need to be mindful of how colleagues might feel if this process seems threatening. Quality Assurance is a check on accuracy, it is not a means of collecting evidence for capability; organisations have different procedures for that.

The main strategy for ensuring accuracy in assessment is known as sampling. In Chapter 3 Quality assurance of assessment you learned that the amount of sampling is dependent on several factors and that there are several ways to prepare sampling plans.

When preparing a sampling plan it is useful to consider your strategy and develop a structure to your plan. One such method uses the acronym **CAMERA**.

CAMERA is a simple means of planning by including a range of scenarios in the sampling plan and creating some principles upon which to validate QA strategies.

–	Candidates
–	Assessors
–	Methods of assessment
–	Evidence or Elements
–	Records
–	Assessment sites

Source: http://www.cityandguilds.com

In this model, the following considerations would be made:

Candidates	Evidence (complete units) from every candidate should be seen at least once during the qualification. This ensures that there is **equality** and fairness between the different candidate characteristics, needs and special requirements. Every candidate should have at least one aspect of their work quality assured.
Assessors	Something from every assessor should be seen at least once during the qualification. The plan would take into consideration the experience of the assessor and the newness or complexity of the qualification. For examples see below. Every assessor should have at least one aspect of their work quality assured. This may occur indirectly through the sampling of **learner** work, but experience may affect the percentage of sampling.
Methods	From the whole of the qualification the plan should include something assessed by each of the different methods of assessment used in the qualification. Particular attention should be given to the use of witnesses or third party assessors when collecting evidence. Every method used to collect candidate evidence should be quality assured during the programme.
Evidence	Evidence types might include electronic or paper versions of evidence collection. You may also see this written as 'elements', although as qualifications are being re-validated the use of elements to break down units or modules is less visible. The expression 'evidence requirements', however, is being seen frequently and IQA should verify against the guidance given. Evidence and assessment relating to 'problem' units would also be offered more scrutiny.
Records	Auditing of records is important to confirm that assessments occur within the registration and that IQA is timely. Dates, signatures, accuracy and compliance are frequent IQA checks when looking at record keeping.

| Assessment sites | Where assessment takes place at different locations, it is important to check consistency of practice across those sites, even if the assessor is the same. On occasions working practices of organisations might impact on a candidate's access to assessment and so this check is required to ensure **fair** access. Every assessment site should be included in the QA sampling plan. |

While CAMERA suggests a methodology, there are other aspects of QA to take into consideration when preparing sampling plans.

Assessor experience An experienced assessor would be one who has assessor qualifications (D32/33, A1/A2 or 6317 Assessment and Quality Assurance), who is occupationally competent (qualified at least to the level above the qualification to be assessed plus trade, industry or professional experience) and is familiar with the occupational standards. While the size of the sample depends upon risk, this might be as little as a 10 per cent sample of their assessment decisions. However, newly qualified assessors working with new qualifications would have a considerably larger sample taken. As the risks associated with accuracy of decisions might be greater, unqualified assessors (working towards assessor and QA qualifications) should have all of their work checked through a countersigning process. Unqualified people, unfamiliar with the occupational standards should be treated as witnesses rather than assessors.

Countersigning This is when an unqualified assessor, who is working towards an Assessment and Quality Assurance qualification, works with an experienced assessor. Every assessment decision they make is checked and countersigned for accuracy. Their candidate's work will then become part of the evidence they require to complete their own qualifications.

Watch point

Ensure that it is clear who has made the assessment decision and who is countersigning that decision.

Communication It is important that the assessment and IQA teams communicate, share ideas and work together to achieve goals. This is more important when assessment is offered away from the main site of the organisation. Sound administrative practice will be required to set up a communication and meeting schedule which is open to all in the assessment and IQA team. Meetings should be minuted and shared among the team. Organisations might need to consider issues around sustainability when arranging meetings and assessments to minimise travel and time demands. Can video conferencing or Skype be used to minimise the impact of excessive travel on the environment?

When to QA? Quality assurance should never be left until the end of the award, although this remains a common practice! QA at this point is 'summative QA'. By undertaking internal quality assessment during the assessment process, any issues relating to inaccurate interpretation of standards, poor practice or non-compliance can be intercepted and resolved before the actions impact on candidate achievement. One way to do this is to assess the assessor assessing. By observing assessment practice IQAs can get a feel of what support assessors need and plan accordingly. Inexperienced assessors might require more internal quality assessment during the process – interim internal quality assessment – thus requiring less summatively.

> ### Watch point
> Identify the problems before they become issues. Don't be frightened to ask for advice. If assessment is going wrong, it is better tackled during the programme than after the candidates have completed it.

Standardisation This process ensures a consistent approach to assessment and agreed standards of working. The concept of standardisation was discussed in Chapter 3 Quality assurance of assessment. Insofar as it relates to internal quality assessment, it is a successful method of preparing assessors prior to undertaking assessments or, alternatively, ensuring that judgements made are consistently applied. Where discrepancies occur, the IQA can arrange additional help, training and guidance to support the assessment team.

One of the benefits of standardisation activities is that of preventing error in assessment practice; consider it risk management. It is a pro-active approach to ensure that assessments are valid and consistent. Another benefit is that of pre-empting problem units. To discuss a unit that is difficult or can be interpreted in different ways is a typical standardisation activity and very helpful to the assessment team. A final benefit is that of agreeing standards of practice – for example: what to ask witnesses to write on their statements? What does a personal statement look like? How much of a programme could be evidenced through recognition of prior learning?

Basic QA planning document

This simple strategy shown below will ensure that something from every candidate is seen at least once during the period of study. It is called **horizontal sampling**. It is the most commonly adopted sampling strategy. By ensuring that every unit or module is subject to QA review, by default, it means that if different units are assessed by different assessors all will be reviewed during the QA period. There are, of course, things that make this process more complex – for example, ensuring that if assessors work on different sites then every site is compared. Similarly, planning must include a strategy to ensure that every assessment method is covered.

| | Start date | Qualification Units/Modules | | | | | | |
		1	2	3	4	5	etc	Date complete
Name	Sep 11	QA Nov11						
Name	Sep 11		QA Dec 11					Feb 12
Name	Jan 12			QA Mar 12				
Name	Jan 12				QA Mar 12			
Name	Jan 12					QA May 12		
etc								

Another method of sampling, known as **vertical sampling** would involve all assessors bringing in a unit to compare practice. For example, each assessor submits unit one, the sampling might investigate how each assessor has assessed the unit, whether problem criteria have been interpreted in the same way, has evidence generated as proof been evaluated in the same way? Are the assessment decisions the same (**reliable**) across the unit and assessors? This would go a long way to prove that your assessment practice offers a fair and equitable service regardless of assessor, location, work experience, etc.

A final sampling strategy, called **themed sampling**, is concerned with themes. In this situation, assessors would produce work assessed by a specific method. Witness testimony is frequently a chosen theme. In this sample the quality assurerwill investigate how each assessor accepts the chosen method, makes reliable judgements on it and confirms the rules of assessment – validity, accuracy, currency and sufficiency. Another frequent theme is one of auditing the date trail. This is a method of ensuring that candidates enrol with the training provider, then with an AO. Then, checking that their assessments are within the period of the programme, allowing time for learning before assessment. Finally, checking that QA dates follow assessment and that there is time for assessors to rectify errors before certification is claimed. This type of activity is also useful in checking that candidates complete in a timely manner, which on Government funded programmes is an essential criteria to secure outcome related funding.

Just a final note in terms of planning. It should also be borne in mind that a plan means exactly that. It is not a 'tablet of stone' and things will impact on the plan.

For example:

- Seasonal influences in horticulture awards will impact on the order the units can be delivered.
- Menus will impact on the completion of catering awards.
- Candidates achieve quicker or slower than expected.
- Sickness of candidates, assessment staff or employers may delay the process.

- Employer's response to business needs create different assessment opportunities.

It is, therefore, important to manage the QA process, prepare for unexpected situations and always record the actual QA date against the planned date.

 ## ACTIVITY 2

Examine the tracker below and decide on your sampling strategy. Explain how you made your decision.

	Start date	**Qualification Units/Modules**						Date complete
		1	2	3	4	5	6	
Eliza Workplace: JB & Co	Sep 11	Ach'd Nov 11 Assr: Sarah	Ach'd Nov 11 Assr: Sarah	Ach'd Nov 11 Assr: Sarah				
Bill Workplace: ABC Ltd	Sep 11	Ach'd Nov11 Assr: Derek	Ach'd Nov11 Assr: Derek	Ach'd Nov11 Assr: Derek	Ach'd Dec11 Assr: Derek	Ach'd Jan12 Assr: Derek	Ach'd Feb12 Assr: Derek	Feb12
Sahid Workplace: ABC Ltd	Jan 12	Ach'd Feb12 Assr: Derek	Ach'd Feb12 Assr: Derek				Ach'd Feb12 Assr: Derek	
SammyJo Workplace JB & Co	Jan 12	Ach'd Mar12 Assr: Sarah					Ach'd May12 Assr: Sarah	
JJ Workplace Ditty & son	Jan 12	Ach'd Apr12 Assr: Goran		Ach'd Mar12 Assr: Sarah	Ach'd Mar12 Assr: Sarah			
Winston JB & Co	Feb12	Ach'd Mar12 Assr: Sarah						

Implementing the quality assurance

Adherence to the organisation's assessment and QA policies is the only way to implement effective QA. The policies are agreed and approved by AOs and are tested in their visits. It is, therefore, essential that whatever arrangements have been planned, they are carried out fully. Failure to do this is the main reason for sanctions from the AOs.

Without repeating too much, the main policy and processes are concerned with:

- Sampling to verify and/or moderate decisions.
- Standardisation to confirm consistency and moderate between assessors.
- Record keeping to create an audit and reference trail.
- Communication to ensure everyone knows what is going on.

This will ensure that inaccuracies are identified quickly and are rectified before they impact on candidate achievement.

Quality Assurance occurring during the assessment process is known as **interim QA**. It is likely to involve looking at assessor practice and talking to candidates. Rarely will it look at evidence, as it is likely to be incomplete, although formative assessment will accurately identify the missing components. As a result, **formative feedback** sessions will either be observed or documentation reviewed.

Simple documents can be used to record any observation of assessment activity or formative feedback sessions.

Assessor:			IQA:
Candidate:			Date:
Standard:		Y/N	Comment:
PLANNING			
Was the assessment planned?			
Did the plan include information about what was to be assessed, how, when, where and who was involved?			

Were appropriate risk assessments in place relevant to the assessment task?		
Was the assessment planned to ensure fair, equitable and reliable assessment?		
Were any special arrangements made to meet candidate needs – e.g. timing, resources and/or support?		
Did the assessment use a standalone or holistic approach?		
Did the candidate understand the proposed assessment process? Was it agreed before being undertaken?		
If others were affected by the assessment or involved in the assessment, did the assessor make relevant arrangements before the commencement of the assessment?		
DELIVERY		
Did the assessor remain unobtrusive, neither helping nor hindering the process?		
Were the standards interpreted correctly?		
Was questioning used? If so, were the questions designed to test knowledge without leading the candidate?		
Did the methods chosen seem the most appropriate for the assessment?		
GIVING FEEDBACK		
Was the feedback provided in a timely manner?		
Was the feedback given in a setting appropriate to candidate confidentiality?		
Did the feedback include a clear statement about the outcome of the assessment?		
Was the feedback constructive?		

RECORD KEEPING		
Were the appropriate documents completed to record the assessment?		

An observation of the assessor can be supplemented by asking candidate's some questions. This will either provide an alternative sampling strategy or complement and/or confirm an existing one. An example of a candidate interview form might look like this:

Candidate	IQA:
	Date:
Question	**Comment:**
How are you involved in the planning of assessments? In what way?	
Do you require any special arrangements when you are assessed? Are these provided?	
Are you given the opportunity to present evidence in different ways, for example, electronically?	
Are you aware of the procedure if you wish to appeal against an assessment decision?	
Is the feedback you are given after an assessment helpful and supportive? Does it provide you with ideas for improving your practice?	
Are you on target to achieve? How do you know?	

A verification strategy, common in written assignment types of assessment is that of verifying the assignment brief before launching to candidates. In this process, the assessors will write the assignment (probably consisting of a number of tasks which collectively evidence the assessment criteria) and submit it to the QA team. In Edexcel programmes this may be the lead internal verifier (LIV). Their role is to check the content of the brief to ensure that it is fit for purpose.

Assessor:		IQA:	
Proposed launch date: Proposed hand-in date:		IQA date:	
Qualification:		Unit/Module:	
QA Check		Yes/No/In part	Comments
Validity			
Do the tasks relate to the assessment criteria of the unit/module?			
Are the tasks at the appropriate level?			
Is the language of the brief relevant to the target group?			
Does the brief offer a fair and equitable opportunity for all candidates to complete the tasks?			
Does any aspect of the task risk contravention of any legislative requirement or moral value?			
Does any aspect of the tasks require additional risk assessments to be undertaken?			
Authenticity			
Does the brief require the candidate to declare that it is their own work?			
Does any part of the assignment require the candidate to reference their citations?			
Currency			
Do the tasks mirror current industry or commercial practice?			
Does the brief require candidates to date their work?			

Sufficiency		
Do the specified tasks cover the content of all assessment criteria in the unit/module?		
Do the specified tasks cover any range requirements? e.g. four types of ...		
Does the brief include reference to functional skills?		
Other		
Is the brief fit for purpose?		
Has the brief been verified prior to issue to candidates?		
Feedback to the assessor		
Areas of good practice: Areas for future improvement: Are any actions required PRIOR to issuing to candidates? Signed: Date:		
I confirm that this brief meets the rules of assessment and organisational policy and that it can be issued to candidates. Signed: Date:		

E-assessment

In Chapter 2 Planning and delivering assessments you looked at the benefits and types of e-assessment tools. This method of storing and collecting evidence provides different challenges in verification and moderation. Quality Assurance systems will need to reflect the method of retrieving and collecting evidence. As well as subject expertise, IQA staff will need to have IT skills and security permissions to access the information, even though the ethos of QA remains the same – checking the validity, authenticity, currency and sufficiency of evidence. Many software programs have systems in-built which record verification activity. In e-assessment, confirming authenticity poses the biggest test, as both the assessor and the QA team need to be confident that the evidence presented is a true demonstration of a candidate's ability. The use of e-signatures needs care to ensure evidence is signed off by the correct person. Authenticity checks can be strengthened through the use of security levels and passwords to limit access to only those with permission to use the software. Additional conversations with assessors, witnesses and candidates as part of the QA process should be carried out to confirm competence and actions recorded in the e-portfolio.

For example:

- Ask candidates questions about the observations and knowledge recorded as achieved to verify competence.
- Ask assessors to confirm visits to candidates and check against assessment dates.
- Ask witnesses what types of statements they have made recently about their candidate's achievements in the workplace.

Watch point

Are you absolutely sure that the evidence is attributed to the candidate? How do you know?

Checking the quality assurance

Lets us now consider what QA staff need to judge when verifying or moderating evidence.

Validity	Is the evidence referenced and linked to the units of assessment? Is the evidence collected appropriate to the qualification? Who has made the assessment decisions – qualified, experienced assessors or others, e.g. expert or non-expert witnesses?
Authenticity	Is there evidence to confirm that it is the candidates own work? Is the evidence signed?

	Do the signatures match the signatures in the 'sample signature' file? Is the assessor competent to make the decision? Is the evidence plagiarised? Have any quotations been accurately referenced using a system like Harvard referencing?
Currency	Has the evidence been collected after the date of registration with the awarding organisation? Has the evidence been collected during the period of enrolment with the training provider? Is the evidence dated? Does the evidence reflect current industry or commercial standards? If RPL is used as an assessment method, then is it recent practice, i.e. derived within the past 12 months (or in line with the assessment strategy)?
Sufficiency	Is there enough evidence to cover the content of the UoA? Is there enough evidence to cover the range of evidence requirements specified in the assessment guidance? Does the evidence provide proof of competence over a period of time?
Reliability	Is the practice consistent across all assessors and locations? Are assessment records accurate and complete? Is evidence stored securely?
Fairness and equity	Do the chosen assessment methods enable access by all candidates regardless of gender, age, ethnic background, disability, marital status, sexual orientation, etc.? Do assessors consider shift patterns and seasonal factors, etc., when assessing evidence?

Acting on and identifying improvements

A vital part of the QA process is concerned with creating opportunities for improvement. There are various stages within the QA process which seem to provide such situations.

Induction is the first opportunity to establish how experienced or confident an assessor is in their duties. It is at this point that certificates will be confirmed. When a new assessor (or IQA) is appointed, their original certificates will be required to be seen by the AO. Generally, this occurs at the first visit where the EQA will view originals and sign copies of the certificates for the centre to keep in its management files. Sample signatures will be taken and stored and appropriate passwords issued to retrieve electronically stored information.

When collecting signatures, it might be pertinent to collect not only the full signature used to sign off assessment, but if the assessor uses initials to sign evidence, then that symbol should also be taken.

At commencement of assessment activity, the assessor should also be given access to information, documentation and records relating to assessment, organisational policy, candidates and employers or training and assessment venues. Ideally this is either stored electronically with an explanation of how it can be accessed or as part of a pack of materials. This information should clearly describe who will be assessed, against what standards, when and where they will be

INDUCTION CHECKLIST			
	Y/N		Y/N
CV		Username and password issued	
Signature – full and initials		Specifications issued	
Original certificates (to be presented at visit on .. /.. /....)		Assessment documentation issued	
Photocopied certificates		QA documentation discussed	
Schedule of standardisation events and meetings issued		Candidates allocated	
Candidate records issued		Assessment sites identified	
Training record established		Mentor/IQA allocated	

assessed, guidance on how those assessments are conducted and all relevant processes. The IQA appointed should take the opportunity to conduct an initial assessment and training needs analysis to establish a solid foundation for the new assessor.

At standardisation and moderation meetings there will be opportunities to review what decisions the assessment team is making. Where there is inconsistency or a lack of compliance, then the IQA will be able to target training and development to those individuals and teams requiring such support.

Ongoing throughout the working life as an assessor, the assessor should update their own personal, professional and vocational practices. This is widely known as CPD. Assessors, who belong to the Institute for Learning (IfL), are required to complete up to 30 hours of CPD per year.

The Institute for Verifiers and Assessors (IVA) is another professional body that uses member subscriptions to organise CPD opportunities.

What constitutes CPD?

Awarding Organisation require assessors and QA staff to engage in CPD activities. Some will specify how many hours per year are required to demonstrate up-to-date practice. CPD activities include:

- development of functional skills – e.g. literacy, mathematics, ICT
- development of personal skills – e.g. time management, problem solving
- development of professional skills – e.g. assessment specific updating
- development of vocational skills – e.g. industry or commercial updating
- development of study skills – e.g. note taking, researching
- development of training skills – e.g. differentiating, planning, e-learning
- development of legislative changes – e.g. copyright, health/safety, equality
- development of support skills – e.g. special educational needs, learner support
- development of skills to embed functional skills into sessions
- awareness of imminent changes in policy or practice
- awareness of new management information systems
- awareness of organisational processes and procedures.

Feedback following quality assurance

One of the most valuable tools to inform improvements is feedback. We read in Chapters 1 The principles of assessment: functions and concepts and Chapter 2 Planning and delivering assessments about the importance of feedback in terms of moving a candidate forward. Assessors are no different. They require feedback to develop and hone their skills. They also need to know when they are doing a good job and can share their good practice.

Feedback to assessors should use the constructive feedback model. These are the aspects of the job that you do well, the areas to improve upon and the suggestions offered to make those improvements. As with many processes, the quality assurer needs to re-visit the feedback and actions to 'close' the action once it has been achieved, i.e. close the loop.

Below are two examples of forms to record QA activity and provide feedback to the assessor. These are important as they both confirm accuracy in assessment and indentify development needs.

Basic QA feedback sheet – Individual feedback

Assessor	
Candidate	
Describe the QA sample:	
Unit/module	
Assessment methods used:	
Location/site of assessment	
Records reviewed	

Did the sample meet the rules of evidence, was it:			
Valid?	Authentic?	Current?	Sufficient?

Feedback to assessor
Was the assessment decision agreed?
Further actions identified
To be completed by (date and by whom)
Actions completed.
Checked by: Date completed:

In this simple form, the IQA is required to check that the assessment decisions are accurate. It also leads the IQA to ensure that there is enough evidence across the range and scope of provision to make a judgement about the confidence in this assessor's decisions. The feedback here is aimed at assessors not candidates so it should be written to reflect the actions an assessor must undertake, either to improve this particular assessment, or their future practice. It should be clear, factual and honest, with constructive and helpful comments. It should identify the strengths and weaknesses of the assessment practice, stating what needs to change and if relevant, identify strategic improvements, i.e. those required over the longer term.

Basic QA feedback sheet – Multiple feedback

In assignment based work there is a tendency to undertake internal quality assurance on a unit and to gather a number of candidate's work to make the QA decisions. An example is shown overleaf.

In this basic form, the IQA would look at a number of samples from submitted work. While each would be checked against the rules of assessment, the **summative feedback** to the assessor would address the whole of the sample. At the planning stage you would ensure that different candidates' work is looked at over the total number of units or modules in the qualification, thus ensuring every candidate, every unit and every assessor is reviewed.

Reflection

Assessors and QA staff are encouraged to be reflective practitioners. At regular points in the assessment and quality cycles it is useful to sit back and review what has transpired.

The cycle of QA is now complete. At this point the process would start again with improved practices in assessment. A revised sampling strategy would be planned to check that the issues identified had been implemented and that there was a discernible impact, namely more rigorous assessment. This would again be checked and further improvements identified and implemented.

Assessor	
Candidate	

Describe the QA sample:
Candidate work on final submission of assignment

Unit/ module	

Did the sample meet the rules of evidence, was it:					
	Valid?	Authentic?	Current?	Sufficient?	Decision agreed
A					
B					
C					
D					
E					

Feedback to assessor

Further actions identified

To be completed by (date and by whom)

Actions completed.
Checked by: Date completed:

ACTIVITY 3

Make a list of three things that have gone particularly well, and three things that have given rise to most concern.

1. ☺

2. ☺

3. ☺

1. ☹

2. ☹

3. ☹

Why do you think the good things went well and what are the circumstances surrounding the not so good bits?

Glossary of terms

Authentic   being the learner's own work

CAMERA   acronym for a suggested sampling strategy

Currency   reflects current or recent work practices

Equality   a state of fair treatment that is the right of all the people regardless of the differences in, for example, culture, ability, gender, race, religion, wealth, sexual orientation, or any other group characteristic

Evidence   the output of an assessment activity; evidence of a learner's knowledge understanding, skills or competence that can be used to make a judgement of their achievement against agreed standards/criteria

Fair   ensuring that everyone has an equal chance of getting an objective and accurate assessment

Formative feedback   on-going feedback to support development

Horizontal sampling   sampling across all units in the programme

Interim QA   quality assurance within the programme designed to support and develop practice

Learner   the person being assessed by the candidate assessor

PICA   acronym for components of the quality cycle; plan, implement, check, action

Reliable   consistently achieves the same results with different assessors and the same (or similar) group of learners

Requirements   these could be the requirements of the practitioners own organisation or those of an external organisation such as awarding organisation

SSC   Sector Skills Council (part of UK Commission for Employment and Skills)

Sufficient   enough evidence as specified in evidence requirements or assessment strategy

Summative feedback   feedback at the end of the unit or programme in which the final judgement is made

Summative QA   quality assurance at the end of the unit or programme

Themed sampling   sampling focused on a specific aspect of assessment

Valid   relevant to the standards/criteria against which the candidate is being assessed

Vertical sampling   sampling of a single units across all assessors

Recommended reading

City and Guilds (2011) *Level 3 and 4 Awards & Certificates in Assessment and Quality Assurance: qualification handbook for centres.* February 2011

Collins, D (2006) *A survival guide for college managers and leaders.* London: Continuum

Hill, C (2003) *Teaching using Information and Learning Technology in Further Education.* Exeter: Learning Matters

Hoyle, D (2007) *Quality Management Essentials.* Oxford: Heinemann (Elsevier)

Sector Skills Councils: UK Commission for Employments and Skills –

Whalley, J, Welch, T and Williamson, L (2006) *E-Learning in FE.* London: Continuum

Wilson, L (2008) *Practical Teaching: a guide to PTLLS and CTLLS.* London: Cengage Learning

Wilson, L (2009) *Practical Teaching: a guide to PTLLS and DTLLS.* Andover: Cengage Learning

Wolf, A (2011) *Review of Vocational Education – The Wolf Report.* March 2011

Wood, J and Dickinson, J (2011) *Quality Assurance and Evaluation.* Exeter: Learning Matters

Useful online resources

Useful references for further reading about assessment are:

http://www.ukces.org.uk/

https://www.education.gov.uk/publications/standard/publicationDetail/Page1/ DFE-00031-2011 (accessed May 2011)

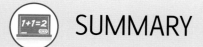 # SUMMARY

In this chapter we set out to:

- Describe the importance and key attributes of planning processes in assuring quality.
- Summarise the main sampling strategies.
- Identify activities which contribute to QA procedures.
- Outline the role feedback has in developing assessment practice.
- Reflect on current practice and plan to develop skills and knowledge.

Your personal development

- You have commenced learning in this chapter by revising assessment practices, originally discussed in Chapter 1 The principles of assessment: functions and concepts and Chapter 2 Planning and delivering assessments. The new information was introduced through 'The Quality Cycle' using the acronym PICA, which stands for plan, implement, check and act.

- In the first section, you studied the importance of the UK Commission for Employment and Skills' role in licensing Sector Skills Councils who set the benchmarks and requirements of QA – both internal to the training organisation and external to it. You may also need to review the importance of legislation and the role of Ofqual to further your understanding.

- You explored the use of CAMERA as a means of establishing a sampling strategy and reviewed each aspect of the expression to consider how each could be sampled.

- You thought about the processes which impact on planning effective internal quality assurance, namely assessor experience, countersigning assessments, communication, and standardisation and then you scrutinised some suggested planning documents. Please note that you should always default to your organisation's agreed documentation, the ones displayed here are only ideas.

- When devising plans, you compared and contrasted the merits of horizontal, vertical and themed strategies of sampling. Hopefully, you have concluded that each has a number of values and that over a period of time all methods should be included to establish a broad range of sampling.

- You then moved on to looking at implementing an internal quality assurance strategy. This section generally reinforced the activities in the planning section earlier, but extended your knowledge by considering the impact of observing the assessors assessing and questioning candidates about the assessment process. Also in this section, you explored the importance of quality assuring assignments briefs before they were issued to candidates to ensure that they were decreed fit for purpose.

- You then had an opportunity to reflect on the specific challenges facing the internal quality assurance team when verifying or moderating e-assessment activity – especially in relation to confirming authenticity.

- The chapter progressed and caused you to focus on the rules of assessment and what actions the internal quality assurance team need to carry out to check that they have been applied consistently and in line with organisational policy and procedures.

- In the final component of this chapter, you evaluated what all of this meant and what the next stage was. You looked at how internal quality assurance is a means to improvement, but equally so are an effective induction, regular standardisation events, constructive feedback mechanisms and the emergent CPD.

- All of the processes together form the quality cycle – a continuous strategy to promote improvement.

In the next chapter we will look at the management of quality assurance in an organisation.

CHAPTER 5

Managing the quality assurance process

Unit of Assessment	Assessment Criteria
Understanding the principles and practices of assessment	No direct links although theory underpins the management of the assessment process
Assess occupational competence in the work environment	No direct links although theory underpins the management of the assessment process
Assess vocational skills, knowledge and understanding	No direct links although theory underpins the management of the assessment process
Understanding the principles and practices of internally assuring the quality of assessment	No direct links although theory underpins the management of the quality assurance process
Internally assure the quality of assessment	No direct links although theory underpins the management of the quality assurance process
Plan, allocate and monitor work in own area of responsibility	1.1; 1.2; 1.3; 1.4; 2.1; 2.2 3.1; 3.2; 4.1; 4.2

LEARNING OUTCOMES

By the end of this chapter you will be able to:

....

- Describe the processes involved in managing the quality assurance of assessment
- Plan for quality assurance management
- Identify the resources required in quality assurance
- Implement and monitor quality assurance in own area
- Organise an external quality assurance activity
- Manage and implement improvements

The management of quality assurance

This chapter is concerned with managing the assessment and QA processes. The chapter will cover aspects in relation to planning, monitoring, improving and providing an impact on actions. The concepts and principles referred to are those previously described in earlier chapters.

O'Connell (2005: 182) describes the management of quality assurance as:

> *'Putting systems in place to ensure that high standards are achieved: as little as possible is left to chance in ensuring "right first time".'*

He states that by being proactive in the approach to QA there will be a more productive outcome than relying on a reactive approach, i.e. discovering problems and putting actions into place to resolve them.

Cole and Kelly (2011: 332) maintain that quality management is both proactive and reactive. They agree that:

> *'Written procedures, instructions, forms or records help to ensure that everyone is not just "doing his or her own thing" and that the organisation goes about its business in a structured way.'*

Effective QA, therefore, starts with procedures and systems to describe the correct way. The manager of the QA process will, therefore, be responsible for ensuring compliance.

Typical procedures seen in the assessment and QA process are:

- assessment policy and procedure
- assessment malpractice procedure
- assessment appeals procedure
- internal QA policy and procedure
- internal QA strategy
- enrolment and registration procedures
- information, advice and guidance policy
- support for learners policy and procedures
- management Information procedures
- equality policy and procedures
- health and safety policy and procedures
- safeguarding policy and procedures.

The management of quality assurance practices

In the context of assessment and QA, this is the tier of the QA process that monitors or manages a particular area of provision or a particular qualification. Those responsible for the management of assessment and QA may be called programme managers or coordinators, IVCs or LIVs. The role may or may not be part of the organisation's (centre's) management structure. In this instance 'management' is perceived as a function as well as a role. For the purpose of clarity, in this chapter people managing the assessment and QA processes will be referred to as lead quality assurers (LQAs). Figure 5.1 attempts to represent a typical organisational structure for an assessment and QA team.

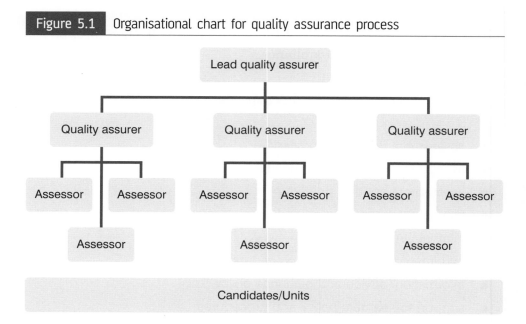

Figure 5.1 Organisational chart for quality assurance process

In essence, the LQA is likely to coordinate a number of internal quality assurers (IQAs) each of whom will be working with a number of assessors. Their role is to standardise, communicate, disseminate and monitor QA practice within their area of coordination. The holder of the role may not necessarily be a subject expert, but will have supervisory or management experience, probably within the broad subject sector area. The structure may be arranged so that assessors are responsible for a number of candidates, each completing a full qualification, or, alternatively, assessors may be responsible for specific units which collectively form a qualification. Quality assurance staff will be appointed to oversee the work of a number of assessors, or specific levels or qualifications. As there is no 'right way', each centre should arrange the structure of its QAs to suit its needs and methods of delivery. The important aspect is that it is clearly described and justified and then agreed with the AOs.

Some AOs are modifying their QA processes to devolve more of the responsibility of compliance and summary sampling to their approved centres. Edexcel introduced the role of LIV in September 2010 to coincide with the launch of the new QCF qualifications. Edexcel, the AO, then samples activity within the centre at a management level and a few qualifications rather than in every subject/qualification area.

As this role is quite obviously a managerial or supervisory role the occupational standards and learning outcomes for this part of the assessor and quality assurance qualifications are taken from the leadership and management standards. These are:

Plan, allocate and monitor work in own area of responsibility:	
1. Be able to produce a work plan for own area of responsibility.	1.1 Explain the context in which work is to be undertaken. 1.2 Identify the skills base and the resources available. 1.3 Examine priorities and success criteria needed for the team. 1.4 Produce a work plan for own area of responsibility.
2. Be able to allocate and agree responsibilities with team members.	2.1 Identify team members' responsibilities for identified work activities. 2.2 Agree responsibilities and SMART (specific, measurable, achievable, realistic and time-bound) objectives with team members.
3. Be able to monitor the progress and quality of work in own area of responsibility and provide feedback.	3.1 Identify ways to monitor progress and quality of work. 3.2 Monitor and evaluate progress against agreed standards and provide feedback to team members.
4. Be able to review and amend plans of work for own area of responsibility and communicate changes.	4.1 Review and amend work plan where changes are needed. 4.2 Communicate changes to team members.

The LQA has a responsibility to manage and oversee the QA and assessment processes by:

- Defining the roles and responsibilities of the team.
- Preparing and implementing the assessment strategy in line with their organisation's assessment policy and procedure.
- Preparing and implementing the QA strategy in line with their organisation's QA policy and procedure.
- Ensuring assessment and QA practice is fit for purpose.
- Creating opportunities to quality assure all aspects of the learner journey.
- Planning QA throughout the assessment process.
- Observing assessment and QA practice.
- Providing support to assessors and QA teams and monitoring CPD activity.
- Implementing standardisation activities to ensure consistency in assessment.
- Ensuring learning and assessment practices meet trainee's needs and aspirations.
- Ensuring learning, assessment and QA practices meet the requirements of the NOS.
- Ensuring learning, assessment and QA practices comply with the SSC's and AO's assessment strategy.
- Communicating effectively with all relevant people.
- Monitoring that all of the above happens in a timely manner and is recorded and reported in line with their organisation's policy.

In order to achieve this, the LQA must have a good grasp of the principles of assessment and QA as well as the skill of management. Aspects of assessment can be found in Chapter 1 and Chapter 2; aspects of QA can be found in Chapter 3 and Chapter 4.

Assessment	Quality assurance	Management
Roles/responsibility	Roles/responsibility	Communication
Criterion based	Regulatory	Decision-making
assessment	requirements	Delegation
Formative assessment	Legislative	Data management
Summative assessment	requirements	Financial
Principles of assessment	Models of QA	management
(consistent, accessible,	Centre approval	Leadership
detailed, earned and	Candidate registration	Problem solving
transparent)	and certification	Target setting
Rules of assessment	Record keeping	Conflict
(valid, authentic,	Sampling strategies	management
current, sufficient,	Standardisation	Planning
reliable)	Inducting and	Motivation and
Assessment language	supporting assessors	feedback
Qualification structure	CPD	
Assessment cycle	Sanctions	
Legislative requirements	Disputes and appeals	
Equality and diversity	Charter marks	
Ethics	Quality cycle	
Disputes and appeals		
Recording keeping		
E-technology		
Assessment methods		
Questioning skills		
Feedback skills		

Resourcing quality assurance

When an organisation commits to delivering a qualification – i.e. becoming an approved centre – it does so by assuring the AO that it has both the physical and human resources required to deliver the qualification with integrity. The role of the LQA is to ensure that this is upheld.

Physical resources covers:

- Traditional resources – teaching and learning materials, access to placements/work, accommodation, paper based resources.
- E-technologies – computer hardware, internet, log-ins, specialist software.

ACTIVITY 1

Using the NOS for your area of work, review the standards to list the resources that are needed to implement training, assessment and QA procedures.

Divide your list into learning/assessment, technological and specialist equipment.

Carry out an audit of your work area – including placements – and prepare a report to confirm suitability of resources including a rationale for any additional requirements.

- Additional support – computerised adaptations, e.g. voice recognition software.
- Specialist equipment – technical machinery, software, equipment to support the learning and assessment of all units of assessment within the qualification.

Human resources covers:

- Qualifications – sufficient qualified assessors and QA staff to meet the learners' needs and availability.
- Experience and skills – assessors and QA staff who meet the role specifications. (See Chapter 1 The principles of assessment: functions and concepts and Chapter 3 Quality assurance of assessment.)

The LQA is responsible for maintaining assessor and QA practitioner profiles and keeping accurate records of the team's CPD.

Each member of staff in the team should complete a profile document to keep in the management file (see Documenting and recording quality assurance management below). This provides an overview of the team and should be updated annually. Staff who are 'working towards' qualifications should be included as the LQA will need to make additional arrangements to support countersigning requirements. For best practice, a similar document should be included in the candidate's portfolio to include people who are signing evidence in their portfolios.

Name	Role	Technical qualification	Professional qualification	Sample signature
	This might be trainer, assessor or QA or combination of all.	List the highest level qualification held relating to the qualification delivered. Inc. Awarding Organisation and year of achievement.	Include training, teaching and assessment or QA qualifications. These should be commensurate with role.	Include a full signature and the mark or initials used on evidence.
For example:				
Joe Bloggs	Trainer & assessor	HND in xxyy (BTEC, 2002) GCSE English (AQA, 1996)	L4 CTLLS (C&G, 2010) A1 (C&G, 2008)	*Joe Bloggs* *(JB)*

Each member of the assessment or QA team should submit an up-to-date CV, their CPD plan, a list of CPD attended during the last 12 months and copies of certificates held. At an External Quality Assurance (EQA) visit, the AO's representative will want to see original certificates; they will then sign the centre's file to confirm 'original seen'. Once validated, the QA will only wish to see updated and recently acquired certificates.

Watch point

A note about certificates:

- Certificates issued by an AO represent nationally recognised qualifications. Assessors are usually required to be qualified to level three in their subject, but experience is also valid – if proven.
- Certificates issued by employers represent in-house qualifications relating to specific methods of working. They may not be transferable.
- Quality assurers will need to make a judgement about the importance of any certification in relation to age, validity and relevance to the target qualification or NOS.

> ● Attendance certificates mean just that; the owner attended the event – it does not mean they listened, learned or were even awake!

The CPD plan should be linked to the comments and actions reported during QA sampling as well as other generic personal, professional and technical updates identified. An example would be:

CONTINUOUS PROFESSIONAL DEVELOPMENT PLAN

COVERING THE PERIOD FROM: 2012–2013

Extract from entries:

Planned CPD activity and date identified	Aims and desired outcomes of activity	Suggested methods to achieve the planned outcomes	Target date for completion	Actions
Performance Development Review: September 2012 Diversity Awareness	To identify key legislation and implications. To raise awareness of impact in lessons. To modify handouts to ensure all are inclusive.	Online diversity package on the Intranet	August 2013	Enrol for programme. To find out how to enrol check with Personnel. Check date of next inset day.
Peer observation Any identified actions	To improve the quality of assessment practice.	Mentor support LQA Advice Standardisation meetings	July 2013	Check with manager before embarking on activities requiring funding.

TARGET CPD HOURS: 30	IfL Membership No: AA123456 Organisation: A N Other Training

Name: *Joe Bloggs*
I agree to support the Continuous Professional Development plans identified above.
Manager's signature: *Ima Boss*   Date: *September 2012*

CONTINUOUS PROFESSIONAL DEVELOPMENT RECORD				
COVERING THE PERIOD FROM: 2012–2013				
Extract from entries:				
Date of event/hours	Nature of event	Why?	What did I learn from this?	How the organisation, teams and I have benefited
27/10/12 7 hours CPD	Diversity Awareness Training Internal online programme of study	Identified in my PDR. This is becoming high profile and all staff are required to attend.	What diversity means, what constitutes discrimination and how it impacts on teachers.	I have been more conscious when devising assessment plans to check for discriminating practices. I will now challenge unacceptable behaviours more confidently; my planning seeks to include a wider variety of experiences. In team meetings we discuss how to create more diversity in the curriculum.
08/02/13 3 hours CPD	Standardisation meeting Research activity	My LQA suggested that my assessment practice could be developed.	Using the internet I found a lot of information about assessment mostly to do with setting clear feedback and future goals.	I ensure that I give each candidate the opportunity to check/identify what evidence they wish or need to present to meet the criteria. At the end of the assessment I set SMART targets for improvement and future actions, which means I can measure their achievement against standards.
TOTAL No CPD HOURS 10 hours	IfL Membership No: AA123456 Organisation: A N Other Training				

Name: *Joe Bloggs*

This document is agreed to be a true record of Continuous Professional Development undertaken.
Manager's signature: *Ima Boss*   Date: *February 2013*

CPD records can be stored in a portfolio type of system, either paper based or electronically. A CPD record should be reviewed annually by a manager or colleague to offer peer support and guidance.

The Institute for Learning (IfL), although the professional body for teachers, is also open to membership from assessors. Members of the IfL have access to RE*f*LECT©, which is an electronic recording system, to plan, record and reflect on CPD opportunities (www.ifl.ac.uk).

Documenting and recording quality assurance management

As established at the start of this chapter, managing the assessment and QA processes is largely a matter of ensuring everyone complies with the procedures laid down by the organisation and when those procedures are compromised, errors will inevitably occur. In this section we look at the documentation that is required to:

- record the outcomes of assessment
- record QA activity

- record compliance to procedure
- record LQA activity.

In the earlier chapters, you will find a number of documents relating to assessment and QA, including:

Assessment

- initial assessment records
- candidate induction record
- assessment plan
- record of observation
- records of oral questions
- written question sheets
- assignment cover sheets
- declaration of authenticity
- feedback to candidates
- candidate achievement tracking sheets
- witness signature sheet
- records of witness testimony

Internal quality assurance

- assessor induction record
- sampling plans
- observation of assessment records
- candidate interview records
- validation of assignment brief
- feedback to assessors
- outcome of sampling records
- standardisation meeting minutes
- appeals and disputes record

Lead quality assurance

- staff profiles

- qualification management information:
  - specifications
  - candidate listings – registrations
  - team structure
  - records of certifications
  - EQA details
  - EQA report and action plan
  - quality improvement plan
  - minutes of meetings
  - copies of QA records
- QA summary.

Records of assessment and QA are auditable documents. An approved centre is required to keep them for at least three years following accreditation. The documents relating to registration, progress monitoring (tracking) and certification should be kept for three years; documents relating to candidate assessment (e.g. candidate work) and QA processes should be retained until the next EQA activity.

Even if a centre is classified as 'direct claims status' it still has to retain portfolios and records for the next EQA monitoring. This offers a challenge for centres:

- Do you return portfolios to candidates and recall them if required for sampling?
- Do you retain everything until the EQA process is complete?

By returning work to candidates, and after all it is their work (!), you alleviate storage problems. Candidates can use their portfolio evidence to secure future learning or employment opportunities. However, if they leave the area or fail to return them, how will your EQA be able to sample evidence?

If you retain the portfolios, even after certification but until the EQA monitoring, where will you keep them?

Possible solutions to resolve this would be:

- Wherever possible scan documentation and store in electronic portfolios. However, many candidates still use paper-based storage for their evidence, in which case …

- When returning paper portfolios, state that they should be kept intact for at least 12 months in case requested for sampling. However, candidates may move or just not realise the importance of the request, so, try the reverse. Retain the work but provide a testimonial for candidates to use offering a reference pending return of their work – and buy a large, secure cupboard!

An ideal solution would be to keep in regular contact with your EQA. External quality assurers are usually practitioners so will understand the dilemma. As each candidate cohort completes, let the EQA have the sampling information:

- name
- date of birth
- registration number
- start date
- assessment site
- assessor name
- IQA name, if sampled
- completion date.

Ask them to indicate which units or portfolios should be retained and which can be returned. This eliminates the recall issue and minimises the storage requirements. High volume centres may be entitled to more frequent 'desk-based' sampling to keep things moving along. The key to this is communication and building up a relationship with your EQA to ensure business efficiency is suited to centre requirements.

What you need to keep

Forms to summarise verification activity across the qualification/period. This is best kept as a spreadsheet which will enable better searching and filtering of information, but the headings should be as shown on the next page.

This chart collects information, which an EQA or LQA can used to prepare sampling at a management level.

Candidate name	Date of birth	Centre enrolment date	Awarding organisation registration number	Awarding organisation registration date	Assessor name	Assessment site/workplace	Assessment methods used	IQA name	Date of last sampling (if applicable)	Unit accreditation or complete qualification	Completion date	Date certificate claimed (if DCS)

A. N. Other Training Co

Qualification title:

Cohort/group: Start date: End date:

By including in this chart whether or not a unit has been internally quality assured, the EQA or LQA can plan to look at both sampled and unsampled materials – this will be in addition to the usual criteria in a CAMERA style of sampling.

- Candidates
- Assessors
- Methods of assessment
- Evidence or elements
- Records
- Assessment sites

Source: http://www.cityandguilds.com

Lead quality assurers should keep a centre, management or QA file. They all mean the same thing, but you may hear any of these expressions. The file keeps information about the programme, the candidates, the staff and process documentation in one place. This may be electronic or paper-based, but needs to be accessible to the team and AO staff. Contents might include:

- list of candidates
- candidate/assessor allocations
- details of work placements and/or employers (location, insurances, contacts)
- risk assessments
- copies of specifications – or links to where they are stored
- centre organisation chart and reporting lines
- list the team and their role within the team
- staff CVs, qualifications, CPD records and sample signatures
- minutes of meetings
- standardisation records
- QA strategy and plans (including justification of sampling ratios)
- verification and moderation records
- EQA contact details and copies of communications
- recent EQA reports and action plans.

Making improvements

An effective QA process which is systematically and consistently applied should result in few errors. Where errors do occur, the LQA needs to decide whether it is a system or procedure fault or a compliance error.

Systems and procedures should be reviewed annually to confirm that they remain fit for purpose. Documents should be checked to ensure that they record the correct issues. Feedback from EQA staff and internal audits will provide an opinion on how effective the process is.

The alternative error of compliance is more about the fault of individuals in following the procedure; you will have to decide if this is due to lack of training or shoddy practices. Each will have a different action to resolve the issue.

How you deal with errors will depend upon the complexity of those errors and the potential negative impact that may result from the error. All errors should result in a clear target to identify the improvement required. SMART target setting is widely considered the appropriate strategy. There are several different words associated with the acronym, but the meaning is clear and the table below explains the concept:

SMART

Specific	Goals that clearly refer to what is expected
Measurable	Goals using verbs and phrases that can be judged
Achievable/ Agreed	Goals that can be succeeded A more powerful expression because it appears contractual
Realistic/ Relevant	Goals that are reasonable, practical and logical Goals that are appropriate and important (Avoid using achievable and realistic because they mean broadly the same thing.)
Time-bound	Goals that express when things must be done by

Many of the improvements within a programme will come from standardising practice and the team striving to make the candidate's experience an efficient and successful process.

Improvements come from assessors and QA staff looking at their current practices and deciding if and how it can be made better.

Problem units/modules Certain criteria in some qualifications cause problems for assessors. This might be in how they are interpreted or in how they might be evidenced. In a standardisation event the team comes together and talks things through. This will lead to a consensus of opinion on how it will be assessed in the future.

Assessment opportunities Assessment methods or procedures are discussed in order to ensure that they are efficient in collecting the correct amount of evidence to cover the evidence requirements specified. This leads to a development and because it is jointly agreed is owned and understood by the team.

However, not all improvement arises from natural development of ideas to promote improved practice. Sometimes through either capability or failure to comply with processes, remedial actions are required to correct errors and bring about improvement.

What might the errors be and how would you action them?

Many of the actions will be around minor issues, for example missing signatures and dates here and there, or documents completed too quickly maybe with some parts incorrectly filled in. These are easily checked and resolved, because they are not fundamental errors. An action plan to the assessor would suffice with a request for a future sample to confirm that the actions have been met. These types of action do not compromise the integrity of the qualification. However, systematic failure to sign and date anything in the candidate's portfolio is a different matter!

In this scenario, SMART Targets might include:

- Check and complete future assessment records to include a signature and date on all pieces of work.
- Identify a set time each week to complete assessment paperwork. Ensure paperwork is completed fully. Submit paperwork for review by the IQA by the end of the month.

At the other end of the scale are assessments which fail to meet the rules of assessment. Look at the following case study examples.

CASE STUDY 1

You identify that old specifications are being used in current assessments. The rules being broken here are VALIDITY and CURRENCY. This compromises the assessment in that the candidate is assessed against standards that are out-of-date and therefore any certificate claimed would be invalid. The annoying part of this scenario is that candidates rely on their assessors to provide them with assessment material and probably do not realise the error. They would do the work asked of them and not realise that there is a problem.

ACTIVITY:

How would you ensure, through QA processes, that the scenario in this example did not occur?

Answer:

When qualifications change, teams should be brought together in briefing and standardisation activities to discuss the changes and develop new assessment materials. Regular standardisation meetings at which all assessors bring examples of assessed work would identify any problems in interpreting standards. Sampling to cover all assessors during the assessment process would also indicate any problems. Sampling should be carried out within the assessment process rather than at the end of it, when an error has more serious consequences. Audit procedures – for example, each assessor to supply pieces of assessed work for review either by peers or an audit team – would further establish the validity of the assessment content.

IQAs should ensure that new assessors or those working remotely have sufficient materials to carry out their roles. This places an importance on induction and the benefit of electronic resources stored on shared servers. If staff are not able to attend standardisation meetings, the IQA should provide additional support.

SMART targets might include:

- Attend the standardisation meeting on 21/09/2012.
- Bring three examples of assessed work to the IQA by next weekend.

CASE STUDY 2

You identify that a significant part of a candidate's work, is 'cut and pasted' from the internet. There is no referencing or statement to say that it is not the candidate's work. The rule being broken here is AUTHENTICITY. This compromises the assessment in that by presenting work that is not their own, an assessor cannot guarantee that the candidate understands the concept or activity that they require an explanation of. If unchallenged both the assessor and the candidate are guilty of cheating or assessment malpractice. The integrity of the qualification and the reputation of the organisation are compromised.

ACTIVITY:

How do you advise your assessors and candidates to reference or cite published information in their work? Is this included in your induction material or candidate information pack?

Answer:

Organise a themed standardisation meeting to look at referencing and assessment malpractice. At the meeting assessors and IQAs should agree the system of referencing to be used – for example Harvard referencing. Develop and distribute a cover sheet (A Declaration of Authenticity) in which the candidate has to declare that 'all the work contained in the assessment/ assignment is my own work and I have acknowledged any sources from published materials'. This should be signed and dated.

A standardisation activity might include an activity in which an unreferenced paragraph is provided and IQAs provide guidance on how to identify whether it is plagiarised or not. There is software available to check work, but the simplest solution is to type the text into an internet search engine. More often than not the plagiarised paragraph appears as the first hit or can be found on an open source website, such as Wikipedia.

Candidate induction should include how to reference published work.

Include in the IQA system a process which requires all bona fide assessors, IQAs, candidates and witnesses to provide a sample signature.

SMART targets might include:

- Complete an induction activity with every new candidate about referencing and the consequences of plagiarism.
- All assessors to countersign the declaration coversheet to confirm that they have checked the authenticity of the candidate's work.

CASE STUDY 3

A candidate has been assessed by observation in their workplace. There is a record of the observation and a record of a few oral questions. All of the documentation is fully completed and the assessor has signed off the unit as complete. However, there is a criterion which is not readily evidenced through natural workplace practice. The rule being potentially broken here is SUFFICIENCY. Rarely do qualifications only require observational evidence. There are usually criteria relating to knowledge and understanding which underpins the practical aspects of the qualification. Unless fully assessed to meet all of the criteria, the assessor is making inaccurate decisions.

ACTIVITY:

How would you use QA practices to ensure that all criteria are assessed correctly? What feedback would you give to the assessor responsible, and what feedback would you give to an IQA if this had gone through a QA process without being identified?

Answer:

Any method of sampling should identify insufficiency of evidence, although in this case vertical sampling would identify it most easily. This is because you will have a number of the same units assessed by different assessors, and will notice different types of evidence being presented. That would alert you to investigating more deeply into why assessors are accepting different types of evidence. Hopefully you would have agreed in a standardisation activity what evidence is typical for particular units, and allowing for minor differences due to different work environments, the evidence base is usually broadly similar. This means that if something is surplus or missing it is quickly noticed. Similarly, units may have a particular criterion that is known to be either problematic in interpretation or in evidencing; consequently you will look at these in detail.

When an assessor reviews evidence, they are checking that the candidate's evidence is sufficient to meet all of the performance and knowledge evidence. In the case above, you would be suspicious in that only performance evidence seems to have been presented and knowing there is a criterion that is not evidenced by observation you would check to see how it has been assessed.

SMART targets might include:

- Arrange to meet the candidate to discuss the issue.
- Resubmit additional evidence in relation to criterion (a) by next week.
- Re-assess the unit and present for QA.

Where issues of weak or poor assessment practice emerge from QA activities, they should always result in an action plan for the assessor. However, some of the issues might be more generic or be concerned with a particular assessor and, therefore, show a lack of consistency. In this case the QA team might want to prepare a Quality Improvement Plan (QIP) for the team. The following example takes the issues in the three case studies above and demonstrates what the QIP might look like.

By preparing a QIP, it provides a mechanism to record issues, note what needs to be done and review frequently to check how well you are progressing. In many organisations this is done quite formally with an independent committee challenging teams on their performance. This has the effect of increasing confidence, promoting responsibility and making people accountable for improvements.

Source	Area for improvement	Success indicator	Actions (SMART)	By whom	By when	Progress
How did you identify it?	Write an evaluative statement about the weakness.	What impact do you expect from the actions?	List what needs to be done to achieve the required impact	Who is responsible for ensuring actions completed?	When must the actions be com-pleted by?	How well are you progressing towards the desired impa
QA activity or EQA activity	Invalid assessment decisions due to wrong specifications being used.	All assessment decisions valid.	Prepare induction pack for assessors to include documents. Arrange six weekly standardisation meetings. Audit all candidate log books for currency. Complete sampling plan to increase % verified.	State who, e.g. LQA.	State dates – do not say 'ongoing.'	Schedule issued to all assessors fo present year. Plans update to increase sampling fror 10% to 20%.
QA activity or EQA activity	Poor referencing practice leads to potential assessment malpractice.	All candidate work attributed as authentic.	Update candidate induction material to include guidance on referencing. Arrange themed standardisation activity. Arrange staff dev. in Harvard referencing. Prepare a declaration of authenticity sheet.	State who, e.g. LQA.	State dates – do not say 'ongoing.'	Scheduled in plan. Speaker contacted. Sheet devisec awaiting approval.

urce	Area for improvement	Success indicator	Actions (SMART)	By whom	By when	Progress
tivity EQA tivity	Inaccurate assessment decisions.	All assessment decisions valid and sufficient to meet specifications.	Modify QA Plan to include vertical sampling. Arrange a standardisation meeting to discuss unit. Allocate additional sampling of named assessor.	State who, e.g. LQA.	State dates – do not say 'ongoing.'	Plan amended. Activity scheduled for next month. Additional QA planned for assessor.

There are many ways of identifying improvement:

● internal quality assurance

● external quality assurance

● audit

● reflection

● self-assessment

● peer review.

Internal and external quality assurance activities are mainly those around standardisation and sampling. An effective IQA process will eliminate potential for poor practice or provide the platform for identifying issues. If issues are discovered by the external QA, it leads the EQA to have less confidence in the approved organisation's ability to lead improvement. This may lead to sanctions on the approved centre.

Audit is a specific activity which looks at aspects of the core business. These may be real or simulated inspections carried out, either by organisations like Ofsted, or consultants or internal teams.

Another method of improvement is to undertake reflective activities, such as self-assessment or peer review. These offer teams the opportunity to be self-critical and identify what needs to happen to improve. The chances are that the same actions would result as those stated on the exemplar QIP above.

However, issues are identified, many of the resultant actions required to make improvements are going to centre on CPD activities. Every assessor and IQA is required – through the SSC's assessment strategy or the approved centre's policies to keep up-to-date and possibly engage in a specified number of hours of training and development. An LQA is, therefore, required to keep records relating to this, as described earlier in the chapter.

Creating an impact

How do you know if what you have done has made any difference? This is a key question. Unless you are able to show an impact on your actions you can't really say if they have improved to the benefit of the candidates or organisation.

In order to ascertain the impact you will need to either:

- use data to show the improvement, or
- seek the views of candidates and assessment teams.

Impact is only relevant if it demonstrates an improvement on the learner experience, financial efficiencies, staff morale. For example: you have worked hard to get all of your documentation into a corporate format; it looks really good and professional. So what? How does this affect candidate achievement? Does it mean you have a healthier recruitment? Unfortunately, this is one valuable improvement that has little impact other than aesthetic. It does not mean that it didn't need to be done; just that it doesn't easily show an impact.

Using and interpreting data and information to demonstrate impact

Organisations, particularly those using public funds, are measured on their success. The data does help in other aspects though, for example it can lead you to required improvements or demonstrate that improvements have had an impact on outcomes.

And now for some numeracy ...

CASE STUDY 4

	Unit Number										
	1	2	3	4	5	6	7	8	9	10	completed
	Assessor: Joe QA: Mary				Assessor: Simon QA: Joe		Assessor: Mary QA: Simon				
Ann	✔	✔	✔	✔	✔	✔	✔	✔	✔	✔	y
Briar	✔	✔				✔	✔				withdrawn
Carrie	✔		✔					✔	✔		
Dena	✔			✔					✔		
Edward	✔	✔	✔	✔	✔	✔	✔	✔	✔	✔	y
Fiona	✔	✔	✔	✔	✔	✔	✔	✔	✔	✔	y
George				✔	✔	✔	✔	✔			
Henry	✔	✔	✔	✔	✔	✔	✔	✔	✔	✔	y
Ingrid	✔	✔	✔	✔	✔	✔	✔	✔	✔	✔	y
Jumar	✔	✔	✔	✔	✔	✔	✔	✔	✔	✔	y
Khalid	✔		✔					✔			
Lucy	✔		✔								withdrawn
Mohamed	✔	✔	✔	✔	✔	✔	✔	✔	✔	✔	y
Norman	✔	✔	✔	✔	✔	✔	✔	✔	✔	✔	y
Oscar	✔	✔	✔	✔	✔	✔	✔	✔	✔	✔	y

✔ = completed units (shaded squares indicate sampled units)

This table can tell us several things:

- how far the candidates have progressed
- the retention percentage
- an achievement rate
- overall success
- the percentage of samplings.

Candidate information

There are 15 candidates in this cohort of the qualification. The qualification consists of 10 units. Nine candidates have completed all 10 units. Two have unfortunately withdrawn from the programme leaving four who have yet to complete.

To calculate the unit progress to date:

To calculate the units achieved as a percentage of the whole the formula is:

Number completed ÷ total units × 100

For example: when Briar withdrew she had completed 4 of the 10 units

4÷10 × 100 = 40%

How near to completion is George?

Answer:
Half way through. George has achieved 5 of his 10 units = 50 per cent

To calculate the retention rate:

Number of candidates at the start − number of candidates leaving
= number remaining
Number remaining ÷ number of starters ×100
= retention rate/percentage

For example: 15 candidates started this programme, 2 have now left therefore there are 13 remaining.

13÷15×100 = 86.6666% (87% to nearest whole number)

Recalculate the retention rate if you find out that Dena no longer wishes to continue

Answer: 80%

(15 - 3 = 12) remaining

(12 ÷ 15) × 100 = 80% retention rate

To calculate the achievement rate:

Achievement is the number of candidates who have achieved the qualification as a percentage of those that remain on the programme.

Number completed ÷ Number retained × 100

For example: 9 candidates from the remaining 13 on programme have achieved the qualification.

9 ÷ 13 × 100 = 69.23% (69% to nearest whole number)

Re-calculate the achievement rate now that Dena has left. What impact does this have on the achievement figure? What conclusions might you draw from this?

Answer: 75%

9 learners have completed, but now only 12 remain on-programme.

9 ÷ 12 = 75%

This has the effect of raising the achievement rate, which initially looks like an improvement.

To calculate success:

Success is the number of candidates who have achieved as a percentage of those that started on the programme.

Number completed ÷ Number of starters × 100

For example: 9 candidates from the original 15 starters have now succeeded in achieving their qualification.

9 ÷ 15 × 100 = 60%

Re-calculate the success rate now that Dena has left. What impact does this have on the success rate? What conclusions might you draw from this?

Answer: No change

However, by Dena withdrawing from the programme there is no chance that she will achieve and therefore the success rate will be lower.

In the original scenario (with 2 leavers) if everyone else achieved the success would be 13 out of 15 = 87%, but Dena leaving means that the maximum success will now be 12 out of 15 = 75%. As many providers and colleges are measured on success, this one learner leaving means a reduction of 12% in the overall success. This is a worrying scenario. By interpreting and predicting this, QA staff can intervene and maybe offer Dena alternative assessment opportunities to ensure her success.

What else does this table tell you?

It tells you what the current percentage of units sampled are against the total required. There are 15 candidates, each with the potential of completing 10 units. This means that there are 150 sampling opportunities. To achieve a 10 per cent sample you should verify 15 units. In this example, 111 units have been completed by the candidates and of those 15 have been sampled.

$$15 \div 111 \times 100 = 13.5\%$$

This tells the LQA that a sufficient QA sample has been applied to this cohort.

What kind a sampling strategy has been used in this example? If each of the candidates had a different assessor, what is the percentage sample size per assessor?

Answer: Horizontal sampling (see Chapter 4 Internally assuring the quality of assessment page 135).

There has been a 10 per cent sample size from every assessor.

ACTIVITY 2

Using the case study above answer the following.

What are the implications if:

Units 1–4 are assessed by Joe, 5 and 6 by Simon and 7–10 assessed by Mary.

Recalculate the sampling percentages per assessor and decide if additional sampling is required.

Answer:

Joe: 15 candidates × 4 units = 60 sampling opportunities. 8 units sampled = 13%

Simon: 15 candidates × 2 units = 30 sampling opportunities. 3 units sampled = 10%

Mary: 15 candidates × 4 units = 60 sampling opportunities. 4 units sampled = 7%

This would indicate that additional sampling is required on Mary's assessments.

Preparing for external quality assurance

The EQA (also known as external verifier) is appointed by the AO to check that approved centres are meeting the requirements of the awarding organisation and is tasked to ensure that Ofqual's standards are being upheld.

The role of the EQA is a valuable part of the quality assurance processes. They have a multiple role; they are both the 'guardian of the rules' and will check that the centre is coping with the managerial,

ACTIVITY 3

Using the case study above answer the following.

The table shows us that Unit 1 has been sampled three times, Units three, four and five sampled twice and the remaining units once each. No unit has been omitted from the sampling strategy. What information can be gleaned from this information?

Answer:

This is very typical in a horizontal sampling strategy, in that there may be variance between the sampling patterns in different units. Overall every candidate has been sampled and every unit is sampled. Either by the strategy that every candidate has a different assessor, or by the scenario above where Joe, Mary and Simon assess different units, this means that the work from all assessors has also been sampled.

The LQA might extend this by undertaking a standardisation activity with Unit 1, to see if the assessment practice is consistent; this would be particularly valuable if there were many different assessors assessing Unit 1, but less so if the same assessor made the decisions alone for this unit.

administrative and practical requirements of assessment and quality assurance. They are also a means of cascading and sharing best practice. They are likely to be working with a number of centres and, as such, will be able to talk about good ideas they have seen on their travels. While maintaining confidentiality about their centres' practices they will pick up tried and tested examples of good assessment and QA practices and are happy to convey them as part of other centres' development. The conversations occurring during EQA activity are therefore invaluable in suggesting actions to improve practice. These informal conversations are the most satisfying part of the role of the EQA. The EQA therefore is the best CPD a centre can access.

In order to raise standards, *'City & Guilds is working to support and guide centres to be better able to assess their own performance and to focus on quality management. The External Verifier role is evolving into a Qualification Consultant role. Because for the future the focus will be to advise, support and guide centres to excellence rather than to "police" standards. City and Guilds believes that "Quality" and "quality" assurance should be built into all activities from the start – it is much easier to build good quality in than to audit poor quality out …'*

Charmain Campbell, City and Guilds 2011

External quality assurance will take place in one of two ways; either by a visit to the centre or remotely through postal or electronic sampling. Increasingly the AO's external quality assurance strategy is based on a risk assessment of the approved centre, this will determine the frequency of EQA activities, but it is usually an annual process. The risk is based on the level of confidence that an AO can place on an approved centre's ability to plan, assess, quality assure and certificate its qualifications.

Whether by a visit or a postal verification, EQA activity should be managed. Once candidates are registered with an AO it will trigger EQA activity.

If this is done by a visit, the activities are likely to be centred on meeting staff and candidates and looking at completed work. The following listing, much of which is contained in a centre management or QA file, can be used as a checklist to prepare for a visit:

Item required at visit	Checked and confirmed
Copy of previous EQA report	
Copy of action plan to show progress of previous actions	
Relevant staff/departments notified of EQA visit	
Copy of pre-visit planner (from EQA) completed and sent to EV	
Confirm dates with EQA	
Base room booked for visit	

Car parking space reserved if appropriate	
Reception notified of EQA arrival date and time	
Check all portfolios and/or logbooks requested for sampling are available for inspection	
Cross check portfolios and/or logbooks for: • date compliance • evidence of assessments • evidence of IQA • all signatures and dates complete • cross referenced to standards, learning outcomes, assessment criteria • evidence of constructive feedback to candidates	
All candidates requested for interview with EQA are available (a telephone appointment is acceptable)	
All assessors requested for interview with EQA are available (a telephone appointment is acceptable)	
Assessor's records/documents available and audited	
All quality assurance staff requested for interview with EQA are available (a telephone appointment is acceptable)	
QA records/documents available and audited	
IQA actions set previously have been closed and signed off	
Minutes of standardisation events, team meetings and attendance at CPD is documented	
If EV requests: has observation of assessment been arranged?	
If necessary, inform candidate's employer that EQA will require a site visit	
Details of team – candidate /unit allocations with sample signatures available	
New team members – CV + original certificates	

Notes regarding preparing for a visit or postal verification:

- Only candidates registered with an AO can be externally verified. Candidates enrolled at a centre but not registered with an AO cannot submit work for verification.

- Any assessments recorded in portfolios or log books which pre-date the AO registration date are not valid.

- An EQA is checking that the IQA process is being applied. This is to ensure that the IQA policy, procedure and guidance are being followed.

- The rules of evidence are: valid, sufficient, authentic and current; ensure that evidence presented by candidates satisfies these rules and assessors can state how they ensure these rules are applied.

- The principles relating to the IQA sample size are that the sample should cover a range of assessments for every candidate, every module/unit, every assessor, the assessor's experience, at every assessment location, over a range of assessment methods. An IQA strategy should be presented to show how the IQA has created the sample and an IQA should be prepared to answer questions on their justification/strategy.

- Documents stored electronically must be available for EQA scrutiny.

- New assessors need to be introduced to the EQA, they should bring with them a CV and original certificates appropriate to the qualification – for example: evidence of occupational experience/ qualifications, assessment and/or verifier certification. An EQA will require copies which will be signed 'original seen' for their files.

- If the activity is a visit then prepare an agenda, remembering to include all meetings requested by the EQA and time and space for the EQA to review paper based or electronic evidence. You will not be required to sit with the EQA for the duration of the visit but should remain close and at the end of a telephone.

- Meetings with candidates, assessors and IQAs ideally are face-to-face interviews. In exceptional circumstances a telephone appointment can be made. In which case the EQA will need access to the phone number and a telephone to make appropriate contacts.

- If preparing a postal verification, then remember that an EQA can only make judgements on what is seen. If you do not send key explanatory documents then you may cause additional work to validate the sample.

The outcome of a successful EQA activity is the confirmation that the approved centre is confident and competent in delivering, assessing and quality assuring its qualifications on behalf of the AO. The role of the LQA in making that happen is paramount, and the sense of satisfaction as the EQA says 'no actions identified' is second to none and worth the effort required to achieve it.

Glossary of terms

EQA   external quality assurer (appointed by an AO)

Learner journey   the learner's experience of an organisation from first to final contact

LQA   lead quality assurer (appointed by an approved centre)

Malpractice   improper or negligent actions

Policy   a statement of proposed actions

Procedure   a way of working

Process   a sequence of activities

Recommended reading

Bush, T and Middlewood, D (1997) *Managing People in Education*. London: Paul Chapman Publishing

City and Guilds (2011) *Level 3 & 4 Awards & Certificates in Assessment and Quality Assurance*. www.cityandguilds.com (version 1.3 February 2011, p. 16 accessed April 2011)

Cole, G A and Kelly, P (2011) *Management Theory and Practice*. Andover:
  Cengage
Collins, D (2006) *Survival Guide for Managers and Leaders*. London:
  Continuum
Ellis, C W (2004) *Management Skills for new Managers*. New York:
  AMACOM
O'Connell, Sir B (2005) *Creating an Outstanding College*. Cheltenham:
  Nelson Thornes
Wilson, L (2009) *Practical Teaching: a guide to PTLLS and DTLLS*.
  Andover: Cengage Learning

SUMMARY

In this chapter we set out to:

- Describe the processes involved in managing the quality assurance of assessment.
- Plan for quality assurance management.
- Identify the resources required in quality assurance.
- Implement and monitor quality assurance in own area.
- Organise an external quality assurance activity.
- Manage and implement improvements.

Your personal development

- You commenced learning in this chapter by considering how the management of the QA process differs from the role of a quality assurer. This caused you to think about how to manage the implementation of QA to ensure that it is procedurally compliant.

- You have explored the role of the LQA and the possible roles and responsibilities the role attracts. You have reviewed how the management of physical and human resources are key to ensuring that QA is effective and carried out with integrity and how this is demonstrated to AOs. In this section you checked that the physical resources were appropriate to the qualification. You evaluated staff experience and qualifications against the requirements of the qualification and AO, touching briefly on CPD and how this is identified, recorded and demonstrated.

- In the next section you looked at documentation and what is required of managers of the QA process. You were reminded of the assessment and QA records originally described in earlier chapters and how you summarise QA activity. You examined a document used by EQA staff which offers an overview of assessment and QA and is used to identify sampling.

- In considering managing the QA process, the next section caused you to reflect on how improvements can occur, and how you can measure the impact of your development actions. This explored SMART target setting and provided several case studies which enabled you to theorise on how you would use QA processes to take development and remedial actions. This led to a review of how QIPs are used to develop and record improvement.

- In the penultimate section, you scrutinised a case study and used numerical statistics to demonstrate how to improve sampling strategies. This same case study was used to calculate retention, achievement and success information and then enable you to conclude that data is deceptive and needs to be carefully analysed to be an effective development tool.

- Finally, you considered how to prepare for an external quality assurance visit and by ensuring that this process is as methodical as others in the QA processes, it will realise a successful outcome, that is: no action points.

In the next chapter you will find help and advice on how to achieve this and other units of your QA award.

CHAPTER 6

Collecting evidence and compiling a portfolio

Unit of Assessment	Assessment Criteria
Understanding the principles and practices of assessment	1.1; 1.2; 1.3; 1.4; 2.1; 3.1; 3.2; 3.3; 3.4; 3.5; 4.1; 4.2; 4.3; 4.4; 5.1; 5.2; 6.1; 6.2; 6.3; 7.1; 7.2; 8.1; 8.2; 8.3; 8.4
Assess occupational competence in the work environment	1.1; 1.2; 1.3; 1.4; 2.1; 2.2; 2.3; 2.4; 3.1; 3.2; 3.3; 4.1; 4.2; 4.3; 4.4
Assess vocational skills, knowledge and understanding	1.1; 1.2; 1.3; 2.1; 2.2; 2.3; 2.4; 2.5; 2.6; 3.1; 3.2; 3.3; 4.1; 4.2; 4.3; 4.4
Understanding the principles and practices of internally assuring the quality of assessment	1.1; 1.2; 1.3; 1.4; 2.1; 2.2; 2.3; 3.1; 3.2; 4.1; 4.2; 4.3; 5.1; 6.1; 6.2; 6.3; 6.4
Internally assure the quality of assessment	1.1; 1.2; 2.1; 2.2; 2.3; 2.4; 2.5; 2.6; 3.1; 3.2; 4.1; 4.2; 5.1; 5.2; 5.3; 5.4
Plan, allocate and monitor work in own area of responsibility	1.1; 1.2; 1.3; 1.4; 2.1; 2.2; 3.1; 3.2; 4.1; 4.2

LEARNING OUTCOMES

By the end of this chapter you will be able to:

- Describe the main features of your portfolio of evidence relating to the assessor and QA qualifications
- Prepare a programme suitable for the delivery of knowledge and understanding
- Develop and accumulate knowledge and understanding evidence
- Aid and support the compilation of your performance evidence to meet the evidence requirements

The assessment and quality assurance qualifications

This chapter of the book refers to the reader as the candidate of the **assessor** and QA **qualifications**. It should be remembered that the **evidence** produced will also be assessed by an assessor and verified by a **qualification quality assurer**. To this end, the person compiling the evidence is referred to as the **candidate assessor** or **candidate quality assurer**. The **principles** of assessment previously described in the rest of this book refer to both the candidate assessor/quality assurer and the **qualification assessor**/quality assurer.

It is this two tier, yet same subject focus, which, in the early stages causes much confusion. In essence, everything you are being asked to complete as part of your assessor or QA qualification, will also be completed by your assessor in their role as a judge of your competence.

Figure 6.1 demonstrates the people involved in the process of achieving assessor and quality assurer qualification/awards. The darker shaded boxes relate to the person registered to complete either the assessor units or the quality assurance units. They are referred to

Figure 6.1 Assessor and quality assurer qualification/awards

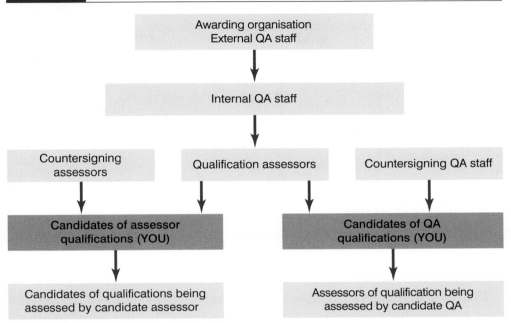

as the candidate assessor or candidate quality assurer. The person assessing you is referred to as the qualification assessor or qualification internal quality assurer – i.e. someone accredited to assess the assessor and quality assurance qualifications.

The candidate assessor will work with **trainees/learners** completing either an accredited qualification or in-house/industry devised training competences. The candidate quality assurer will work with assessors of either accredited qualifications or industry devised training competences. In this context the word 'qualification' is used but applies to both categories.

What constitutes evidence?

Evidence is defined as the output of an assessment activity; evidence of a learner's knowledge and understanding, skills or **competence** that can be used to make a judgement of their achievement against agreed standards/criteria. In this section we take a look at the evidence that would be required of someone completing an assessor or internal QA qualification. Evidence collected by candidate assessors and quality assurers can be:

- observation of performance
- oral questions
- written questions
- products, documents, artefacts, photographs, video clips, records
- professional discussion
- personal statements or logs, reflective accounts
- witness **testimony**
- supplementary evidence – i.e. that which contextualises or explains the context of other pieces of evidence.

Each of these is discussed as an assessment method in Chapter 2 Planning and delivering assessments, pages 44–53 and can be stored as a **portfolio** – either in a folder or electronically. (See also Chapter 2 Planning and delivering assessments, pages 66–67 – Portfolios).

Unfortunately, it is not possible for an assessor or candidate to just say 'I do that'. They need to be able to prove it.

An artist or model has used a portfolio for many years; it being a collection of pictures or images to prove their ability and versatility. A qualification portfolio is exactly the same; it is a collection of proof.

Observation of performance Candidate assessors will be observed by their qualification assessor while working with their trainees/candidates; candidate quality assurers will be observed by their qualification assessors while undertaking activities relating to internal monitoring of quality requirements. Your qualification assessor will observe (listen) while you give feedback to your trainees/learners or assessors – dependent upon the qualification you are working towards. This would be planned in advance in order to ensure that you can alert your trainees/learners/assessors and their employer to the fact that additional people will be watching the process.

Oral questions These will probably be asked following an observation. They will be asked to clarify something seen during the observation or to confirm something related to it. They will probably start 'what would you do if ...' or 'can you explain why ...'. Oral questions are not exclusively part of an observation; you and your assessor may select this method of testing knowledge evidence. Your assessor will need to record the question and your answer. The assessor may record on a document, voice recorder or by video. You may use Skype if it is not convenient to meet with your assessor. You must include the evidence that questioning has occurred in your portfolio.

Written questions These are likely to be pre-set by your qualification assessor and used to confirm your knowledge and understanding. Typically questions may be short answer type, written in such a way so that you can demonstrate your understanding of aspects of the qualifications – especially those not observed or evidenced by producing products. They are unlikely to be tests or exams with time constraints – many will allow the use of texts to complete the questions (i.e. open book questions). There are two sets of suggested pre-set written questions below which may help in your gathering of evidence for either the assessor or internal QA qualifications.

Products, documents, artefacts, photographs, video clips, records
Work products are items, for example, business/service documents (minutes, print-outs, forms, procedures, diagrams); finished goods, commodities or commissions; or anything similar produced during normal work activities. For a candidate assessor these are likely to be things like assessment plans or records of progress/achievement related to your assessments. For a candidate quality assurer they are likely to be minutes of meetings, verification documents, procedures or other products relating to your QA actions. You should obtain authorisation to use any document or procedure. If using mobile technology to video an assessment or take photographs of learners, you must ensure that appropriate permissions are sought and received before using them in your evidence. This would demonstrate awareness of safeguarding procedures and data protection requirements.

Watch point

Policies – what do they prove? Do not encourage policies as evidence – it is more appropriate for the candidate to make a statement or engage in discussion about how they apply the policy. Including policy documents says more about the candidate knowing where to find them rather than how to use them!

ACTIVITY 1

Locate the Policy for Assessment or Internal Quality Assurance at your place of work. Write a statement about how you use or apply either of those policies in your area of work.

Professional discussion This is when you and your qualification assessor engage in conversation about a topic. In some parts of your qualification, it is not possible to cover all of the evidence requirements by observation. In these circumstances you talk to your qualification assessor about how you would, for example, use RPL or case studies as assessment methods. This is likely to be a structured conversation and the qualification assessor may ask specific questions or direct the discussion in a particular direction. You should prepare for a professional discussion. Plan with your assessor the types of topics you will cover and practise what you want to say. You may need to provide documentary evidence to support your statements. You professional discussion will be noted or recorded to provide a record of the conversation.

Personal statements or logs, reflective accounts These can be used as an alternative to professional discussion. Whereas a discussion involves you and your qualification assessor, in statements you write how you do (or would do) something. For example, you might use personal statements to demonstrate your knowledge of legislation or equal opportunities in situations – especially those that were not observed. You might use them to describe how you prepare **contingency plans** or meet specialist requirements of some learners. A statement should be referenced to a particular topic rather than a rambling piece of text about general issues.

Witness testimony A witness is someone who is able to **testify** (validate) that they have seen you do something. A witness might be one of your learners or their employer, or for a candidate quality assurer, one of your assessors. They will testify to things such as effective communication in the planning of assessment or QA. As a candidate assessor/quality assurer your assessments need to be confirmed by a qualified assessor who is a subject expert. This is known as **countersigning**. Because you are in training (to be an assessor or quality assurer) you will find this support invaluable in deciding if evidence is to the required standard, i.e. meets the rules of evidence (valid, authentic, current and sufficient). The countersigning of decisions made by candidate assessors or candidate quality assurers is part of many SSCs' assessment strategies.

You will find these the most commonly used methods of assessment when completing your qualification. You will produce evidence relating to the performance evidence – i.e. evidence of you doing the job. This forms half of the evidence, the rest being derived from knowledge evidence – i.e. what you understand about the job. Acquiring knowledge of the subject is most likely to be by attending some training sessions. Personally, I find that learning about assessment and quality assurance (the theory) is best when it precedes the application. Therefore, I would do a training session before embarking on a task. Others may find the theoretical aspects easier to comprehend after they have done the tasks, allowing them to 'hang'

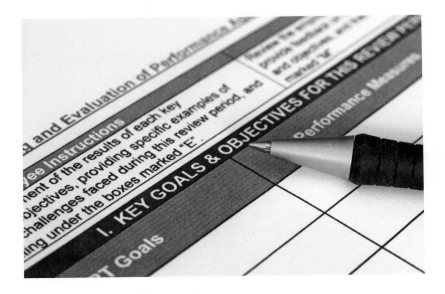

their knowledge onto actions. The order is less important than the fact that both aspects need to be completed to create a deep understanding and proficient application of the roles. Your preference should be discussed as part of your personal development plan when embarking on the chosen qualification.

Evidence requirements

In order to achieve the units you need to collect the following evidence.

Unit 301: Understanding the principles and practices of assessment

This unit is assessed by assignments, written questions or professional discussion. There is no requirement to be assessing trainees in their workplaces as the content of this unit is concerned with the theory that underpins assessment practice. It is a unit suitable for practising assessors or those seeking to become assessors.

Unit 302: Assess occupational competence in the work environment

To achieve this unit you can be assessing trainees/candidates/learners attempting qualifications or in-house/industry or organisational standards. In the first instance:

- Identify two trainees/learners who are currently being assessed in the workplace. To provide a broader range of evidence, one of these trainees/learners should require special arrangements to enable them to work towards their qualifications.

- Plan two assessments for each **trainee/learner**. These four assessments can be on the same day with one following the other, but they must be separate assessments with a planned and complete process for each.

- Arrange for your qualification assessor to observe at least one of the briefings for each trainee/learner with the others evidenced by witness testimony.

- Undertake the assessments – all four must be observed by your qualification assessor. During the four assessments you should use observation, examination of work products and questioning – you do not need to use them all in each observation, but overall they should all be observed by your assessor. A statement is required to show how you would plan and execute other methods – discussion, use of testimony, personal statements, RPL. At least one assessment must include an observation of you giving feedback to your trainee/learner.

Collect all documentation used during the four assessments: plans, observation and assessment records, feedback to trainees/learners, and assessment outcome. See Figure 2.1. To confirm the accuracy of the judgements, the evidence should be countersigned by an accredited assessor who is a subject expert, and ideally quality assured. Your qualification assessor will supply documentation relating to their observation of you, i.e. plans, observation, records of questioning, feedback, and assessment outcome.

Submit additional personal statements, written questions and/or transcript of professional discussion to complete the evidence requirements.

Unit 303: Assess vocational skills, knowledge and understanding

To achieve this unit you can be assessing trainees/candidates/learners attempting qualifications or in-house/industry or organisational standards. In the first instance:

- Identify two trainees/learners who are currently being assessed in contexts other than the workplace (e.g. workshop, classroom, simulated environment, distance/virtual learning environment, area at work away from main work space). To provide a broader range of evidence, one of these trainees/learners should require special arrangements to enable them to work towards their qualifications.

- Plan two assessments for each trainee/learner. These four assessments can be on the same day with one following the other, but they must be separate assessments.

- Arrange for your qualification assessor to observe at least one of the briefings for each trainee/learner with the others evidenced by witness testimony.

- Undertake the assessments – all four must be observed by your qualification assessor. During the four assessments you should use a minimum of three methods of assessment from: simulation, skills test, oral/written questioning, assignment, project, case study, RPL – you do not need to use them all in each observation, but overall your chosen methods should be observed by your assessor. For some methods your assessor will observe you 'managing an assessment'. A statement is required to show how you would plan and execute the remaining methods. At least one assessment must include an observation of you giving feedback to your trainee/learner.

Collect all documentation used during the four assessments: plans, assessment records, feedback to trainees/learners, and assessment outcome. See Figure 2.1. To confirm the accuracy of the judgements, the evidence should be countersigned by an accredited assessor who is a subject expert, and ideally quality assured. Your qualification assessor will supply documentation relating to their observation of you, i.e. plans, observation, record of questioning, feedback, and assessment outcome.

Submit additional personal statements, written questions and/or transcript of professional discussion to complete the evidence requirements.

Unit 401: Understanding the principles and practices of internally assuring the quality of assessment

This unit is assessed by assignments, written questions or professional discussion. There is no requirement to be quality assuring the assessor or their trainees in their workplaces, as the content of this unit is concerned with the theory that underpins QA and assessment practice. It is a unit suitable for practising quality assurance staff or those seeking to become QA staff.

Unit 402: Internally assure the quality of assessment

To achieve this unit you can be assessing assessors delivering qualifications or in-house/industry or organisational standards. In the first instance:

- Identify two assessors who are currently assessing at least two candidates each through part of a qualification or in-house/industry or organisational standards. To provide a broader range of evidence, one of these assessors should be less experienced than the other and therefore require more support as they work through their qualifications.

- Plan moderation activities relating to the two assessors, including, managing assessment risk, standardisation and sampling activities (interim and summatively). Collect planning documentation. An example of a sampling plan is seen in Chapter 4 Internally assuring the quality of assessment page 135.

- Collect records relating to the two assessors, including, CV, occupational certificates, CPD logs and feedback resulting from internal QA.

- Arrange to be observed while your assessors are engaged in QA activities.

Collect all documentation used during the QA (moderation, verification) activity. See Figure 4.1. This should include interim QA – for example observing the assessment process, and summative QA – for example reviewing and evaluating assessment products. To confirm the accuracy of the judgements, the evidence should be countersigned by an accredited quality assurer who is a subject expert, and ideally externally quality assured. Your qualification assessor will supply documentation relating to their observation of you, i.e. plans, observation, feedback and assessment outcome. Examples of QA/verification documents are seen in Chapter 4 Internally assuring the quality of assessment pages 139–142.

Undertake a standardisation activity and submit minutes of the meeting, records relating to decisions made and feedback, advice and support given. Arrange for your qualification assessor to observe at least one feedback session to one of your assessors with the other evidenced by witness testimony.

Submit additional personal statements, written questions and/or transcripts of professional discussion to complete the evidence requirements.

Unit 403: Plan, allocate and monitor work in own area of responsibility

Identify the area of work that you are responsible for. The 'work' is the QA practices that are supervised. A personal statement will describe this. This will be in the context of your LIV/quality assurer role. The success criteria are those that will demonstrate effective QA, for example, no or few actions identified in EQA visits, success data and acceptable standards of practice.

The work plan will be the sampling plan the lead verifier creates to ensure effective and efficient QA and assessment practice.

Describe the team in this area and their responsibilities. This might be an organisation chart with role and job descriptors, showing other QA, assessor and trainee allocations. In this context the resources are the assessors and their competence as well as the physical resources required to assess the target qualifications. Additional evidence will come in the style of individual plans and records relating to the IQA and assessor team, job descriptions or work schedules. These will contain targets and deadlines which need to be written in a SMART way.

Collect documentation relating to: the setting of SMART work targets for the team; minutes of meetings; monitoring progress and performance; giving feedback; arranging/delivering CPD; and other improvement mechanisms. You may need to describe how annual performance reviews or developments plans aid the monitoring of performance and lead to improvements.

Provide testimony to demonstrate effective contacts. An observation of a team event would provide evidence of effective communication, advice and support to the team.

Knowledge and understanding

In the following section you will find some questions which will help you to demonstrate your knowledge and understanding of the assessor and IQA qualifications. They also address the additional requirements of the 'best practice' statements. Written questions can be completed as an activity in their own right or used as part of a professional discussion, or a combination of both.

Questions for the assessor qualifications, comprising:

Unit 301: Understanding the principles and practices of assessment

Unit 302: Assess occupational competence in the work environment

Unit 303: Assess vocational skills, knowledge and understanding

QUESTIONS FOR UNITS 302, 302 AND 303

C&G Ref.	Question	Answers to include:
301.1.1 301.1.2	Describe the main functions and principles of assessment?	Initial assessment, formative and summative assessment Making judgements against the rules of assessment – valid-authentic – current – sufficient. Fairness and objectivity.
301.1.3	What are the key roles and responsibilities of an assessor?	Interpreting standards, planning and carrying out assessments, communicating, making judgements about assessments, recording and giving feedback about assessments, attending standardisation and CPD events.
301.1.4	What role do the AO and SSCs have in regulating assessment practice?	The role of Ofqual in setting the regulations The role of the SSCs in writing NOS, UoA and Assessment Strategy. The role of the AO in writing and upholding standards in assessment.
301.2.1 302.1.1 302.2.1 303.1.1 303.1.2 303.2.1 301.4.3 302.4.3 303.4.3	Choose four assessment methods and compare the strengths and limitations of each. Explain how self- and peer assessment promotes learner involvement. Evaluate the assessment methods used in your assessments.	Choose from: observation, reviewing products, **professional discussions, personal statements, recognising prior learning**, simulations, tests, oral and written questions, assignments and projects, case studies, **witness testimony.** Aids preparation and timing of assessment and empowers the learner. (Choosing the emboldened four will also meet parts of 302, others if used should be evaluated to confirm they were most appropriate and comply with assessment strategy.)

C&G Ref.	Question	Answers to include:
301.3.1 302.1.3 303.2.2 301.4.1 301.4.2	List the main factors to consider when preparing assessment plans. Why do you need to involve the learner and others in planning?	What, when, where, how of assessment. Arrangements for dealing with special requirements (e.g. support needs, shifts, not reassessing, normal work opportunities). Communicating with others about the plans. Raised awareness leads to transparency and efficiency in assessment.
301.3.2 301.3.3 302.1.4	What are the benefits of creating holistic assessments and how would these be planned?	Efficiency of assessment covering more than one unit Linking work practice to assessment rather than the other way around.
301.3.4 301.3.5	What are the main risks that an assessor needs to consider when planning and delivering assessment, and how might they be minimised?	Health and safety, stress, malpractice, over-assessment, unfairness, not adhering to assessment strategy. Ensuring planning considers all of these issues and complies with the rules of assessment.
301.5.1 301.5.2 302.2.2 303.2.3 303.2.4 303.2.5	How do you make judgements about competence?	Rules of assessment. Using criteria. Liaise with others. Consider equality of opportunity. Comply with assessment strategy. (Testimony from a subject specialist should corroborate this statement.)
301.6.1 301.6.2 302.2.3	Briefly outline the main QA processes and how your assessments conform to standardised practice.	Sampling, standardisation, fairness, reliability to ensure consistency and credibility.
301.6.3	Describe the process a learner would follow if they wanted to appeal against an assessment judgement.	Informal and formal stages. When to involve the IQA and EQA. How standardisation activities can limit the risk of unfair assessment.

C&G Ref.	Question	Answers to include:
301.7.1	What is the purpose of assessment records? How are assessment records stored? How frequently would they be completed?	To provide points of reference which are accurate and accessible. To support feedback to trainee/ learner. To aid quality processes. Records should be made in a timely manner and available to the trainee, assessor, IQA and EQA.
301.7.2	How does feedback and questioning support trainees/learners?	Aids progression. Provides opportunity to clarify issues. Feedback needs to be constructive. Questions should not lead or hinder attainment.
301.8.1 301.8.3 302.3.3 302.4.1 302.4.2 303.3.3 303.4.1 303.4.2	What are the main pieces of legislation and procedure that need to be considered in your subject area? How do you comply with them?	Legislation: Health and Safety, Equality Act (E&D), Data Protection, Children Act, specialist legislation. Procedure: confidentiality, record keeping, compliance to assessment strategy. Security of information.
301.8.2	How do/might you use e-assessment or technology in your subject area?	E-portfolios, mobile technology, internet, blogs, VLEs, video/audio evidence – flip cams, recordings, etc. On-line testing.
301.8.4 302.4.4 303.4.4	What reflections have you made during this process? What CPD activities have you engaged in?	Personal development plan, feedback from others, standardisation meetings. Personal and professional development – inc. occupational updates.

Questions for the IQA Qualifications, comprising:

Unit 401: Understanding the principles and practices of internally assuring the quality of assessment

Unit 402: Internally assure the quality of assessment

QUESTIONS FOR UNITS 401 AND 402

C&G Ref.	Question	Answers to include:
401.1.1 401.1.2	Describe the main functions and principles of internal quality assurance.	Credibility, respect, ensuring and monitoring quality, compliance, accuracy and consistency, managing risk, identifying cpd, supporting assessors, promoting improvement. Planning, sampling, standardisation.
401.1.3	What are the key roles and responsibilities of an internal quality team?	Roles of IQA (and also – trainer, expert/non-expert witnesses, independent assessors). Involvement in ensuring and monitoring quality of planning, delivery and assessment outcomes.
401.1.4	What role do the AO and SSCs have in regulating assessment and quality practices?	The role of Ofqual in setting the regulations. The role of the SSCs in writing NOS, UoA and assessment strategy. The role of the AOs in writing and upholding standards in assessment and QA.
401.2.1	Explain the benefits of planning IQA activities.	How QA reduces risks relating to accuracy, validity, fairness and consistency.
401.2.2 401.2.3	Describe what an IQA plan should include and what arrangements need to be made to prepare for QA.	Includes: timeframes relating to sampling – interim and summatively, monitoring assessment, standardisation, supporting assessors and minimising risk. Sampling to meet **CAMERA** Arrangements: collating info, communicating.

C&G Ref.	Question	Answers to include:
401.3.1	Compare and contrast a range of sampling strategies and explain what considerations you make regarding deciding upon sample sizes.	Vertical, horizontal and themed sampling. Observing assessors, candidate interviews, discussions with witnesses, sampling products and records. CAMERA, experience, difficult units, size of provision, current assessment activity.
401.3.2	How do you make judgements about the quality of assessment?	Rules of evidence. Using criteria. Liaise with others. Consider equality of opportunity. Comply with assessment strategy. (Testimony from a subject specialist should corroborate this statement.)
401.4.1 402.2.2 402.2.4 402.2.5 402.3.1	Describe how you support assessors. Explain how you evaluate assessor competence. What types of things might you need to feedback to assessors?	Feedback to assessors (not learners). Constructive feedback. Detailed inductions and ongoing support. Development plans. Protocols or strategies to determine experience of assessors. Observing assessors giving feedback. Checking reliability of assessments. Confirming appropriateness of assessments.
401.4.2 402.2.6	How do you maintain consistency in assessment decisions?	Standardisation activities. Recording outcomes of standardisation. Making improvements and agreeing actions following standardisation. Comparing assessments across units, assessors and themes.
402.2.3	What do you look for in your assessors planning and how do you decide if that planning is appropriate?	Special assessment needs. Documentation. All key components of an assessment plan completed. Validity in assessment against the criteria. Planning will lead to sufficient evidence to meet criteria and range.

C&G Ref.	Question	Answers to include:
401.4.3	Describe the process a learner would follow if they wanted to appeal against an assessment judgement.	The role of the IQA in informal and formal stages. Liaising with assessors and when to involve the EQA. How standardisation activities can limit the risk of unfair assessment.
401.5.1 401.6.1 401.6.4 402.5.1 402.5.2	What are the main pieces of legislation and procedure that needs to be considered in your subject area? How do you comply with them?	Legislation: Health and Safety, Equality Act (E&D), Data Protection, Children Act, specialist legislation. Procedure: confidentiality, record keeping, compliance to assessment strategy. Security of information.
401.6.2	How do/might you quality assure assessments collected using e-assessment or technology in your subject area? How do/might you support assessors using e-assessment?	E-portfolios, mobile technology, internet, blogs, VLEs, video/audio evidence – flip cams, recordings, etc. On-line testing. Virtual standardisation. Electronic communication.
401.6.3 402.5.3 402.5.4	What reflections have you made during this process? What CPD activities have you engaged in?	Personal development plan, feedback from/to others, standardisation meetings. Personal and professional development – inc. occupational updates and current assessment/ QA practice.

Additional questions for those undertaking Unit 403: Plan, allocate and monitor work in own area of responsibility are listed overleaf.

QUESTIONS FOR UNIT 403

C&G Ref.	Question	Answers to include:
403.1.1 403.1.2 403.1.3	What do you consider when preparing to work with IQAs and assessors?	Skills of team, workloads of team. Recency/age of qualifications. Experience of assessors and IQA team. Previous EQA reports. Audit outcomes.
403.3.1	What strategies do you employ to monitor progress of the assessment and IQA team?	Standardisation meeting and records. Sampling of work. 1:1 discussions – appraisals, etc. Observing and questioning practice. External and internal audit. CPD events – Personal development plans. Written and verbal communication. IQA/Assessment feedback. Testimony from others.

Putting it together

This section explains what you need to do with all of this evidence in order to achieve the qualifications. When compiling your portfolio you need to consider how the evidence relates to the assessor or QA qualifications, including the additional 'best practice' requirements.

- *Collect* – either chronologically, by subject or by unit (but keep an index to avoid repetition).
- *Reflect* – review what you have collected and choose want to keep; identify missing parts and plan for how you will collect them.
- *Connect* – link to the standards (your assessor will help with this).

Whether your portfolio of evidence is stored in a substantial file or folder, an e-portfolio or portable storage device, it should be clear and tracked to the criteria of the qualification being attempted. You should also check with your tutor about the use of plastic wallets in paper based portfolios – some providers like them, some hate them. If used, you should balance the one piece of paper per wallet with the overstuffed wallets that burst out their contents!

The portfolio needs to be clearly accessible by the owner, the assessor, the IQA and the EQA. Try to avoid the strategy of putting everything in, in case it might be useful.

> **Watch point**
>
> Good quality evidence rather than high volumes of evidence makes for happy assessors!

Incomplete or poorly referenced portfolios will be rejected at assessment or quality assurance on the grounds that the evidence is not easily located and therefore makes it difficult to prove competence.

Suggested portfolio content:

- Title page, including the owner's name and qualification title.
- Index of contents.
- A tracking sheet – linking evidence pages to the standards (referencing), this should also indicate when one piece of evidence is linked to more than one assessment criteria (cross-referencing).
- List of witnesses and sample signatures of those involved.
- Personal information – CV, copies of certificates.
- A contextual statement is useful in understanding who the owner is and the context in which the evidence has been collected.
- The evidence – records of observations, records of questioning, products, personal statements.

Tracking your evidence

An example of a tracking sheet is shown on the next page.

In this example, the candidate assessor has produced evidence of assessment and has been observed relating to one of the four assessments required to sufficiently cover this unit. This grid gives a flavour of how one piece of evidence meets more than one criterion and

Name: A Candidate					Date: 20th November 2012											
Unit: Assess occupational competence in the work environment																
Ref	Evidence	LO 1				LO 2				LO 3			LO 4			
	Learning Outcomes	1.1	1.2	1.3	1.4	2.1	2.2	2.3	2.4	3.1	3.2	3.3	4.1	4.2	4.3	4.
1	Assessment Plan 1	✔		✔	✔								✔			
2	Observation 1					✔			✔				✔	✔		
3	Feedback and Assessment Records 1							✔	✔	✔			✔	✔		
4	Witness Testimony re communication with learner prior to assessment		✔													
5	Work Products – email		✔													
6	Personal Statement re assessment methods not used	✔				✔										
7	Personal statement evaluating methods used														✔	
8	Written Questions/ Professional Discussion			✔	✔	✔	✔	✔			✔		✔	✔		✔

that each criterion is evidenced at least once. A tracking sheet similar to this should be presented towards the start of the portfolio. The centre will provide this document. If evidence is stored electronically, then the 'Ref' column should indicate the file name where the evidence is located. These grids need to be signed and dated by your assessor when they agree that the evidence you have presented does in fact meet the claimed criteria. You would sign and date them also, as would the IQA if they have sampled this unit.

Preparing for the delivery of knowledge and understanding

This section is particularly useful to those delivering assessor and quality assurer awards to candidates. You will find a scheme of work (programme or agenda) relating to the two knowledge units – one to underpin the assessor qualifications and one for the QA qualifications.

Assessor qualification

Scheme of work for knowledge unit – understanding the principles and practices of assessment

The following scheme of work is a suggestion for how the content of this unit might be broken down and delivered to candidate assessors. It requires a minimum of 24 hours of **guided learning hours (GLH)**. It assumes 12 sessions of 2 hours duration, but this may vary according to organisational need. There is also an assumption that this unit is delivered to a group rather than an individual. It would need to be modified if that were not the case. The detailed content would be planned according to the specific preferences and needs of the learning cohort, with teaching and learning methods arranged accordingly.

Prior to the commencement of the programme, the potential candidate assessors should receive appropriate advice and guidance. This may include assessments relating to acquisition of English skills and other diagnostic assessments in order to identify levels of support required.

UNIT 301 SCHEME OF WORK

Session	Content	Extension/assessment activity	Links to Unit 301
1	Introduction to unit and course; ice breaker and introductions. Issue course handbook (assessor qualification). The language of assessment: understanding the terminology. The roles and responsibilities of the assessor and the assessment team (suggested activity: thought shower the duties and summarise into: roles, responsibilities and characteristics).	Prepare a dictionary of terms with their meanings. Locate and save/print (probably from the internet) a copy of the NOS, units of assessment or in-house standards for your subject area. Collect or review a copy of the qualification/ course or student handbook for the qualification/training programme you are to assess.	1.1 1.3 1.4
2	Key concepts and rules of assessment. Legislation and regulation (suggested activity: each group researches a piece of legislation and offers key findings to other groups). Policy and procedure, why do we need them?	Locate and print/save a copy of your organisation's assessment policy and procedure. OR Review an example of an assessment policy and procedure.	1.1 1.2 1.4 8.1
3	Assessment methods – traditional and e-assessment techniques. Questioning techniques. Risks and barriers to assessment. Special assessment requirements (suggested activity: thought shower key barriers to assessment and identify a strategy to support each).	Create a list of the main assessment methods used to collect knowledge and performance evidence for your subject area assessments. Review four methods in detail and identify the main strengths and weaknesses of the chosen methods.	2.1 3.4 3.5 4.4 8.2

Session	Content	Extension/assessment activity	Links to Unit 301
4	Planning assessments – key components of an assessment plan. Holistic v unitised assessment. Preparing for assessment – how to prepare the candidate; liaising with others in the assessment process; peer and self-assessment as an indicator of readiness and development needs.	Collect a copy of your organisation's document for planning assessment. OR Review a planning document. Download the assessment strategy for your subject area (from the AO). Describe a holistic assessment to cover a number of units from a chosen set of occupational standards.	3.1 3.2 3.3 4.1 4.2 4.3
5	Practice workshop Using a set of occupational standards, prepare plans using appropriate assessment methods. Recap – rules of assessment.	Compare and contrast methods and offer suggestions to modify practice to suit: learner with communication barriers; learner who lacks confidence; learner with limited access to assessment opportunities.	5.1 5.2
6	Making assessment judgements and giving feedback (suggested activity: role play feedback models and examples). Record keeping.	Collect copies of your organisation's documents for recording assessment and feedback. OR Review examples of recording documents.	7.1 7.2

Session	Content	Extension/assessment activity	Links to Unit 301
7	Disputes and appeals. Assessment etiquette: confidentiality. E-technology – demonstration of e-portfolio. E&D: meeting the needs of individuals.	Locate your organisation's appeal procedure. OR Review an appeals procedure (for example from an AO).	6.3 8.1 8.2 8.3
8	Brief outline of QA process – what is QA, key practices: moderation and verification: sampling, standardisation, grading.	Collect or review samples of assessed work and annotate to show how it meets the rules of assessment. Attend and collect minutes from a standardisation meeting or simulate a standardisation meeting in class.	5.1 5.2 6.1 6.2
9	Preparing for professional discussion. Create appointment schedule for next week/s.	Prepare personal statements. OR Recap main theoretical aspects of the qualification. Review Chapter 1 The principles of assessment: functions and concepts and Chapter 2 Planning and delivering assessments of *Practical Teaching: A Guide to Assessment and Quality Assurance.*	
10	Professional discussions.	Prepare own discussion topics.	All

Session	Content	Extension/assessment activity	Links to Unit 301
11	Either professional discussions continued or extension activities.	Review evidence requirements for your qualification and prepare evidence for your qualification.	All
12	Reflection. Key learning. Making improvements to practice. Next steps.	Create a personal development plan. Identify key areas for improvement.	8.4

Internal quality assurance qualification

Scheme of work for knowledge unit – Understanding the principles and practices of internally assuring the quality of assessment

This scheme of work is a suggestion about how the content of this unit might be broken down and delivered to candidate quality assurers. It requires a minimum of 45 hours of guided learning. It assumes 15 sessions of 3 hours duration, but this may vary according to organisational need. There is also an assumption that this unit is delivered to a group rather than an individual. It would need to be modified if that were not the case. The detailed content would be planned according to the specific preferences and needs of the learning cohort, with teaching and learning methods arranged accordingly.

Prior to the commencement of the programme, the potential candidate quality assurers should receive appropriate advice and guidance. This may include assessments relating to acquisition of English skills and other diagnostic assessments in order to identify levels of support required.

Session	Content	Extension/assessment activity	Links to Unit 401
1	Introduction to unit, course: ice breaker and introductions. Issue course handbook (internal quality assurance qualification). The language of QA: understanding the terminology. The roles and responsibilities of the IQA and the assessment team (suggested activity: thought shower the duties and summarise into role – responsibilities – characteristics).	Create a mini job description for the role of IQA and link to others in the team (link to Unit 403).	1.1 1.3
2	Recap assessment principles and rules of assessment.	Review Chapter 1 The principles of assessment: functions and concepts and Chapter 2 Planning and delivering assessments of *Practical Teaching: A Guide to Assessment and Quality Assurance*.	1.1 1.2 3.2
3	The functions of IQA. Suggested activity: thought shower purpose of QA. Key concepts, principles and rules of QA. Legislation and regulation including confidentiality. (suggested activity: each group researches a piece of legislation and offers key findings to other groups). Policy and procedure, why do we need them?	Create an information leaflet for a new assessor about the role of IQA. Locate and print/save a copy of your organisation's QA/verification/ moderation policy and procedure. OR Review an example of a QA policy and procedure.	1.1 1.2 1.4 5.1 6.1 6.2

Session	Content	Extension/assessment activity	Links to Unit 401
4	Overview of internal quality assurance strategies: sampling, standardisation, moderation, verification. QA in e-assessment.	Collect examples of IV documentation or review samples of IV documentation.	1.2 2.1 6.2
5	Planning for internal quality assurance (what, why, how, when). Identify the key risk points. The rules of assessment and their relationship to QA.		2.1 2.2 2.3 3.2
6	Sampling models. (suggested activity: prepare exemplar IQA plans and justify the chosen strategy against CAMERA).	Justify how QA models of sampling can lead to effective and efficient assessment.	3.1
7	Preparing for a standardisation meeting. Note taking. Communication and chairing meetings.	Simulate or undertake a Standardisation meeting.	2.2 2.3 4.2
8	Feedback from formative and summative assessment. (Suggested activity: role play or case study examples of weak assessment requiring feedback.) Supporting and inducting assessors.	Prepare an induction plan for a new assessor.	4.1 6.3
9	Dealing with appeals and disputes. Referral to EQA if necessary. Equality and diversity: dealing with and developing assessment to meet the needs of individuals. IQA strategies to standardise and moderate difference.	Locate your organisation's appeal procedure. OR Review an appeals procedure (for example from an AO).	4.3 6.4

Session	Content	Extension/assessment activity	Links to Unit 401
10	Keeping records. Using or developing documentation to lead to accurate and complete IQA practices. Review legislation to ensure transparency in record keeping.		5.1 6.1
11	Preparing for an EQA visit. Internal and external audit. Communication between centres and AOs. Keeping AOs informed.		
12	Preparing for professional discussion.	Review Chapter 3 Quality assurance of assessment and Chapter 4 Internally assuring the quality of assessment of *Practical Teaching: A Guide to Assessment and Quality Assurance*.	
13	Professional discussions.		All
14	Either professional discussions continued or extension activities.		
15	Reflection. Key learning. Making improvements to practice. Next steps.	Create a personal development plan. Identify key areas for improvement.	6.3

Deliverers of programmes, maybe using the suggested programmes above, should ensure that content and activities address the evidence guidelines stated in the AO's published material.

Glossary of terms

Assessor a person in the workplace or other learning environment who is quality assured by a candidate quality assurer

CAMERA acronym for a suggested sampling strategy (candidate, assessor, method, evidence, records, assessment site)

Candidate assessor a person seeking to achieve an assessor qualification

Candidate quality assurer a person seeking to achieve the QA qualification

Competence knowledge of or ability to do something

Contingency plan planning for the unexpected occurrence

Countersign a guarantee of reliability in assessment decisions, made by unqualified assessors

Evidence the output of an assessment activity; evidence of a learner's knowledge understanding, skills or competence that can be used to make a judgement of their achievement against agreed standards/criteria

Guided learning hours (GLH) the number of hours of direct contact required to deliver a qualification

Portfolio a storage tool, used either paper based or electronically to collect evidence

Principle a set of values or beliefs; a rule or moral code

Qualification a set of specifications (units of assessment) leading to an award, certificate or diploma of achievement; an accredited QCF, NQF or NVQ qualification or in-house/industry or organisationally devised set of standards used to assess the competence of trainees/learners

Qualification assessor a person accredited to assess assessor and quality assurance qualifications

Qualification quality assurer a person accredited to quality assure assessor and quality assurance and QA qualifications

Testify/testimony   to bear witness to; to concur; to give evidence of

Trainee/learner   a person in the work place or other learning environment who is assessed by the candidate assessor

Recommended reading

City and Guilds (2011) Level 3 and 4 Awards and Certificates in Assessment and Quality Assurance – Qualification handbook for centres. Qualification: 6317. February 2011

Useful online resources

Developing a portfolio of evidence: www.eoedeanery.nhs.uk

 # SUMMARY

In this chapter we set out to:

- Describe the main features of your portfolio of evidence relating to the assessor and quality assurance qualifications.
- Prepare a programme suitable for the delivery of knowledge and understanding.
- Develop and accumulate knowledge and understanding evidence.
- Aid and support the compilation of your performance evidence to meet the evidence requirements.

Your personal development

- Having established the tiers of assessment and comprehended who is who and who does what in terms of

QA, assessors, candidate assessors/quality assurers and trainees, you started this stage of learning by exploring the meaning of the word portfolio and are now able to describe what it is, what it consists of and how it is compiled. You have looked at evidence of competence and understand the difference between performance and knowledge evidence and how these are demonstrated in your portfolio. You completed this section by confirming your understanding of some key assessment methods for this qualification – observation, oral and written questioning, work products, professional discussion, personal statements and witness testimony.

- Then you considered a suggested programme or scheme of work to gain sufficient knowledge to meet the standards. The topics included in the scheme are explored in detail in the previous chapters (Chapters 1 to 5). If you are reading this as an assessor of the asessor and QA awards you have considered how these could be translated into learning sessions.

- In the next part, you discovered what you need to do in order to achieve the qualification. The main findings here are that to gain the assessor qualification you need to work with two trainees, each doing two assessments. You need to follow a complete cycle of assessment for each of the four assessments – see Figure 2.1, page 39. For the QA qualification, you need to work with two assessors, each of whom has two trainees. Each assessor should complete a full cycle of the 'quality cycle' – see Figure 4.1, page 129. Both units require additional evidence to supplement the performance evidence (best practice evidence) as well as evidence to confirm knowledge and understanding.

- This part of the chapter followed on by making some suggestions regarding what the supplementary and knowledge evidence should consist of. These are written as questions but can be evidence by simply answering them, by using them to reference some personal statements or as a focus for a professional discussion with your qualification assessor.

- Finally, you looked at how all of this is put together and tracked (referenced to the assessment and learning outcomes). The final stage of your development is concerned with doing the job. Your qualification assessor at your chosen centre will support you in achieving your goal.

Good luck!

Appendices

Appendix A: Occupational sectors – Sector subject areas (SSAs)

	Area – First Tier		Area – Second Tier
1	Health, Public Services and Care	1.1	Medicine and Dentistry
		1.2	Nursing and Subjects and Vocations Allied to Medicine
		1.3	Health and Social Care
		1.4	Public Services
2	Science and Mathematics	2.1	Science
		2.2	Mathematics and Statistics
3	Agriculture, Horticulture and Animal Care	3.1	Agriculture
		3.2	Horticulture and Forestry
		3.3	Animal Care and Veterinary Science
		3.4	Environmental Conservation
4	Engineering and Manufacturing Technologies	4.1	Engineering
		4.2	Manufacturing Technologies
		4.3	Transportation Operations and Maintenance
5	Construction, Planning and the Built Environment	5.1	Architecture
		5.2	Building and Construction
		5.3	Urban, Rural and Regional Planning
6	Information and Communication Technology	6.1	ICT Practitioners
		6.2	ICT for Users
7	Retail and Commercial Enterprise	7.1	Retailing and Wholesaling
		7.2	Warehousing and Distribution
		7.3	Service Enterprises
		7.4	Hospitality and Catering
8	Leisure, Travel and Tourism	8.1	Sport, Leisure and Recreation
		8.2	Travel and Tourism

9	Arts, Media and Publishing	9.1	Performing Arts
		9.2	Crafts, Creative Arts and Design
		9.3	Media and Communication
		9.4	Publishing and Information Services
10	History, Philosophy and Theology	10.1	History
		10.2	Archaeology and Archaeological Sciences
		10.3	Philosophy
		10.4	Theology and Religious Studies
11	Social Sciences	11.1	Geography
		11.2	Sociology and Social Policy
		11.3	Politics
		11.4	Economics
		11.5	Anthropology
12	Languages, Literature and Culture	12.1	Languages, Literature and Culture of the British Isles
		12.2	Other Languages, Literature and Culture
		12.3	Linguistics
13	Education and Training	13.1	Teaching and Lecturing
		13.2	Direct Learning Support
14	Preparation for Life and Work	14.1	Foundations for Learning and Life
		14.2	Preparation for Work
15	Business, Administration and Law	15.1	Accounting and Finance
		15.2	Administration
		15.3	Business Management
		15.4	Marketing and Sales
		15.5	Law and Legal Services

Source: Ofqual http://www.ofqual.gov.uk/files/sector_subject_areas_with_ indicative_content.pdf, for a complete version, including the detailed topics within each area and sub-area tiers.

Appendix B: Units of assessment (City & Guilds)

Understanding the principles and practices of assessment

1. Understand the principles and requirements of assessment	1.1 Explain the functions of assessment in learning and development. 1.2 Define the key concepts and principles of assessment. 1.3 Explain the responsibilities of the assessor. 1.4 Identify the regulations and requirements relevant to assessment in own area of practice.
2. Understand different types of assessment method	2.1 Compare the strengths and limitations of a range of assessment methods with reference to the needs of individual learners.
3. Understand how to plan assessment	3.1 Summarise key factors to consider when planning assessment. 3.2 Evaluate the benefits of using a holistic approach to assessment. 3.3 Explain how to plan a holistic approach to assessment. 3.4 Summarise the types of risks that may be involved in assessment in own area of responsibility. 3.5 Explain how to minimise risks through the planning process.
4. Understand how to involve learners and others in assessment	4.1 Explain the importance of involving the learner and others in the assessment process. 4.2 Summarise types of information that should be made available to learners and others involved in the assessment process. 4.3 Explain how peer and self-assessment can be used effectively to promote learner involvement and personal responsibility in the assessment of learning. 4.4 Explain how assessment arrangements can be adapted to meet the needs of individual learners.

5. Understand how to make assessment decisions	5.1 Explain how to judge whether evidence is: • sufficient • authentic • current. 5.2 Explain how to ensure that assessment decisions are: • made against specified criteria • valid • reliable • fair.
6. Understand quality assurance of the assessment process	6.1 Evaluate the importance of quality assurance in the assessment process. 6.2 Summarise quality assurance and standardisation procedures in own area of practice. 6.3 Summarise the procedures to follow when there are disputes concerning assessment in own area of practice.
7. Understand how to manage information relating to assessment	7.1 Explain the importance of following procedures for the management of information relating to assessment. 7.2 Explain how feedback and questioning contribute to the assessment process.
8. Understand the legal and good practice requirements in relation to assessment	8.1 Explain legal issues, policies and procedures relevant to assessment, including those for confidentiality, health, safety and welfare. 8.2 Explain the contribution that technology can make to the assessment process. 8.3 Evaluate requirement for equality and diversity and, where appropriate, bilingualism in relation to assessment. 8.4 Explain the value of reflective practice and continuing professional development in the assessment process.

Assess occupational competence in the work environment

1. Be able to plan the assessment of occupational competence	1.1 Plan assessment of occupational competence based on the following methods: ● observation of performance in the work environment ● examining products of work ● questioning the learner ● discussing with the learner ● use of others (witness testimony) ● looking at candidate statements ● recognising prior learning. 1.2 Communicate the purpose, requirements and the processes of assessing occupational competence to the learner. 1.3 Plan the assessment of occupational competence to address learner needs and current achievements. 1.4 Identify opportunities for holistic assessment.
2. Be able to make assessment decisions about occupational competence	2.1 Use valid, fair and reliable assessment methods including: ● observation of performance ● examining products of work ● questioning the learner ● discussing with the learner ● use of others (witness testimony) ● looking at candidate statements ● recognising prior learning. 2.2 Make assessment decisions of occupational competence against specified criteria. 2.3 Follow standardisation procedures. 2.4 Provide feedback to learners that affirms achievement and identifies any further implications for learning, assessment and progression.
3. Be able to provide required information following the assessment of occupational competence	3.1 Maintain records of the assessment of occupational competence, its outcomes and learner progress. 3.2 Make assessment information available to authorised colleagues.

	3.3 Follow procedures to maintain the confidentiality of assessment information.
4. Be able to maintain legal and good practice requirements when assessing occupational competence	4.1 Follow relevant policies, procedures and legislation for the assessment of occupational competence, including those for health, safety and welfare. 4.2 Apply requirements for equality and diversity and, where appropriate, bilingualism, when assessing occupational competence. 4.3 Evaluate own work in carrying out assessments of occupational competence. 4.4 Maintain the currency of own expertise and competence as relevant to own role in assessing occupational competence.

Assess vocational skills, knowledge and understanding

1. Be able to prepare assessments of vocational skills, knowledge and understanding	1.1 Select methods to assess vocational skills, knowledge and understanding which address learner needs and meet assessment requirements, including: ● assessments in simulated environments ● skills tests ● oral and written questions ● assignments ● projects ● case studies ● recognising prior learning. 1.2 Prepare resources and conditions for the assessment of vocational skills, knowledge and understanding. 1.3 Communicate the purpose, requirements and processes of assessment of vocational skills, knowledge and understanding to learners.

2. Be able to carry out assessments of vocational skills, knowledge and understanding	2.1 Manage assessments of vocational skills, knowledge and understanding to meet assessment requirements. 2.2 Provide support to learners within agreed limitations. 2.3 Analyse evidence of learner achievement. 2.4 Make assessment decisions relating to vocational skills, knowledge and understanding against specified criteria. 2.5 Follow standardisation procedures. 2.6 Provide feedback to the learner that affirms achievement and identifies any further implications for learning, assessment and progression.
3. Be able to provide required information following the assessment of vocational skills, knowledge and understanding	3.1 Maintain records of the assessment of vocational skills, knowledge and understanding, its outcomes and learner progress. 3.2 Make assessment information available to authorised colleagues as required. 3.3 Follow procedures to maintain the confidentiality of assessment information.
4. Be able to maintain legal and good practice requirements when assessing vocational skills, knowledge and understanding	4.1 Follow relevant policies, procedures and legislation relating to the assessment of vocational skills, knowledge and understanding, including those for health, safety and welfare. 4.2 Apply requirements for equality and diversity and, where appropriate, bilingualism. 4.3 Evaluate own work in carrying out assessments of vocational skills, knowledge and understanding. 4.4 Take part in continuing professional development to ensure current expertise and competence in assessing vocational skills, knowledge and understanding.

Understanding the principles and practices of internally assuring the quality of assessment

1. Understand the context and principles of internal quality assurance	1.1 Explain the functions of internal quality assurance in learning and development. 1.2 Explain the key concepts and principles of the internal quality assurance of assessment. 1.3 Explain the roles of practitioners involved in the internal and external quality assurance process. 1.4 Explain the regulations and requirements for internal quality assurance in own area of practice.

2. Understand how to plan the internal quality assurance of assessment	2.1 Evaluate the importance of planning and preparing internal quality assurance activities.
	2.2 Explain what an internal quality assurance plan should contain.
	2.3 Summarise the preparations that need to be made for internal quality assurance, including:
	  ● information collecting
	  ● communications
	  ● administrative arrangements
	  ● resources.

3. Understanding techniques and criteria for monitoring the quality of assessment internally	3.1 Evaluate different techniques for sampling evidence of assessment, including use of technology. 3.2 Explain the appropriate criteria to use for judging the quality of the assessment process.
4. Understand how to internally maintain and improve the quality of assessment	4.1 Summarise the types of feedback, support and advice that assessors may need to maintain and improve the quality of assessment. 4.2 Explain standardisation requirements in relation to assessment. 4.3 Explain relevant procedures regarding disputes about the quality of assessment.
5. Understand how to manage information relevant to the internal quality assurance of assessment	5.1 Evaluate requirements for information management, data protection and confidentiality in relation to the internal quality assurance of assessment.

▶

6. Understand the legal and good practice requirements for the internal quality assurance of assessment	6.1 Evaluate legal issues, policies and procedures relevant to the internal quality assurance of assessment, including those for health, safety and welfare. 6.2 Evaluate different ways in which technology can contribute to the internal quality assurance of assessment. 6.3 Explain the value of reflective practice and continuing professional development in relation to internal quality assurance. 6.4 Evaluate requirements for equality and diversity and, where appropriate, bilingualism, in relation to the internal quality assurance of assessment.

Internally assure the quality of assessment

1. Be able to plan the internal quality assurance of assessment	1.1 Plan monitoring activities according to the requirements of own role. 1.2 Make arrangements for internal monitoring activities to assure quality.
2. Be able to internally evaluate the quality of assessment	2.1 Carry out internal monitoring activities to quality requirements. 2.2 Evaluate assessor expertise and competence in relation to the requirements of their role. 2.3 Evaluate the planning and preparation of assessment processes. 2.4 Determine whether assessment methods are safe, fair, valid and reliable. 2.5 Determine whether assessment decisions are made using the specified criteria. 2.6 Compare assessor decisions to ensure they are consistent.
3. Be able to internally maintain and improve the quality of assessment	3.1 Provide assessors with feedback, advice and support, including professional development opportunities, which help them to maintain and improve the quality of assessment. 3.2 Apply procedures to standardise assessment practices and outcomes.

4. Be able to manage information relevant to the internal quality assurance of assessment	4.1 Apply procedures for recording, storing and reporting information relating to internal quality assurance. 4.2 Follow procedures to maintain confidentiality of internal quality assurance information.
5. Be able to maintain legal and good practice requirements when internally monitoring and maintaining the quality of assessment	5.1 Apply relevant policies, procedures and legislation in relation to internal quality assurance, including those for health, safety and welfare. 5.2 Apply requirements for equality and diversity and, where appropriate, bilingualism, in relation to internal quality assurance. 5.3 Critically reflect on own practice in internally assuring the quality of assessment. 5.4 Maintain the currency of own expertise and competence in internally assuring the quality of assessment.

Plan, allocate and monitor work in own area of responsibility

1. Be able to produce a work plan for own area of responsibility	1.1 Explain the context in which work is to be undertaken. 1.2 Identify the skills base and the resources available. 1.3 Examine priorities and success criteria needed for the team. 1.4 Produce a work plan for own area of responsibility.
2. Be able to allocate and agree responsibilities with team members	2.1 Identify team members' responsibilities for identified work activities. 2.2 Agree responsibilities and SMART (specific, measurable, achievable, realistic and time-bound) objectives with team members.

▶

3. Be able to monitor the progress and quality of work in own area of responsibility and provide feedback	3.1 Identify ways to monitor progress and quality of work. 3.2 Monitor and evaluate progress against agreed standards and provide feedback to team members.
4. Be able to review and amend plans of work for own area of responsibility and communicate changes	4.1 Review and amend work plan where changes are needed. 4.2 Communicate changes to team members.

Source: City & Guilds, 2010

AO	Awarding organisation
APA	Accreditation of prior achievement
APL	Accreditation of prior learning
BTEC	Trade mark for Edexcel qualifications
CADET©	Consistent, accessible, detailed, earned, transparent (acronym for principles of assessment)
CAMERA	Candidate, assessor, method, evidence, records, assessment site (acronym for a suggested sampling strategy)
CCEA	Council for the Curriculum, Examinations and Assessment
CIF	Common inspection framework
CPD	Continuous professional development
CRB	Criminal Records Bureau
CV	Curriculum vitae
DCELLS	Department for Children, Education, Lifelong Learning and Skills
DCS	Direct claims status
DELTA	Disability, Emotional, Language, Technology, Ability (acronym to remember barriers to learning and assessment)
EE	External examiner
EFQM	European Foundation for Quality Management
EM	External moderator
EQA	External quality assurance/assurer (appointed by an awarding organisation)
EV	External verifier
GLH	Guided learning hours

GOLA	Global online assessment
HE	Higher education
HSE	Health and Safety Executive
IA	Independent assessor
IAG	Information, advice and guidance
IfL	Institute for Learning
IiE	Investors in Excellence
IiP	Investors in People
IM	Internal moderator
IQA	Internal quality assurer/assurance
IQAC	Internal quality assurance co-ordinator
IQER	Integrated quality enhancement review
ISA	Independent safeguarding authority
ISO	International Organization for Standardization
IV	Internal verifier
IVA	Institute for Verifiers and Assessors
IVC	Internal verification co-ordinator
LIV	Lead internal verifier
LLUK	Lifelong Learning UK – SSC – disbanded March 2011
LQA	Lead quality assurer (appointed by an approved centre)
MCQs	Multiple choice questions
NOS	National Occupational Standards
NQAI	National Qualifications Authority of Ireland
NQF	National Qualifications Framework
NVQ	National Vocational Qualification
Ofqual	Office of the Qualifications and Examinations Regulator
Ofsted	Office for Standards in Education
OSCA	Online support for centre assessors
PPE	Personal protective equipment
PICA©	Plan, implement, check, action (acronym to remember the stages of the quality cycle)
QA	Quality assurance

QAA	Quality assurance agency
QCF	Qualifications and Credit Framework
QIP	Quality improvement plan
RPL	Recognition of prior learning (formerly APL/E/A – accreditation of prior learning or experience or achievement)
SAR	Self assessment report
SMART	Specific, Measurable, Achievable, Relevant, Time bounded (acronym for target setting)
SMARTER	Specific, Measurable, Achievable, Relevant, Time-bounded, Ethical, Reviewed (extended acronym for target setting)
SQA	Scottish Qualifications Authority
SSC	Sector Skills Council
TNA	Training needs analysis
TQM	Total quality management
TQS	Training quality standard
UoA	Units of assessment
UPK	Underpinning knowledge (theory of a subject)
VBS	Vetting and barring scheme
VDU	Visual display units (in relation to display screen equipment regulations)
VLE	Virtual learning environment

Glossary

A

Accredited a qualification written under Ofqual regulations

Appeal a request to reconsider a judgement made

Assessment the checking of learning and demonstrating competence

Assessor a person in the workplace or other learning environment who is quality assured by a candidate quality assurer

Authentic being the learner's own work

Awarding organisation (AO) a body approved by Ofqual to create and certificate qualifications

B

Bilingualism speaking two languages

C

CADET© consistent, accessible, detailed, earned, transparent principles of assessment

CAMERA candidate, assessor, method, evidence, records, assessment site (acronym for a suggested sampling strategy)

Candidate assessor a person seeking to achieve an assessor qualification

Candidate quality assurer a person seeking to achieve the quality assurance qualification

Certification a process of claiming a certificate following successful completion of a qualification

Closed questioning limited response type of questions

Competence knowledge of or ability to do something

Concept an idea

Contingency plan planning for the unexpected occurrence

Continuous professional development (CPD) on-the-job training for staff

Countersign a guarantee of reliability in assessment decisions, made by unqualified assessors

Criterion (pl: criteria) a standard of competence

Cross reference linking evidence to more than one aspect of the qualification

Currency reflects current or recent work practices

D

DELTA disability, emotional, language, technology, ability (acronym to remember barriers to learning and assessment)

Direct claims status a high level of confidence from an AO, resulting in the ability to claim certification without a visit from an EQA (DCS)

Dispute a difference in opinion of an outcome

Diversity acknowledging that each individual is unique and recognising our individual differences in for example, culture, ability, gender, race, religion, wealth, sexual orientation, or any other group characteristic

E

EQA external quality assurer (appointed by an AO)

Equality a state of fair treatment that is the right of all the people regardless of the differences in, for example, culture, ability, gender, race, religion, wealth, sexual orientation, or any other group characteristic

Evidence the output of an assessment activity; evidence of a learner's knowledge understanding, skills or competence that can be used to make a judgement of their achievement against agreed standards/criteria

F

Fair ensuring that everyone has an equal chance of getting an objective and accurate assessment

Feedback verbal or written comments about the assessment intended to bring about improvement

Formative assessment interim or ongoing assessment

Formative feedback on-going feedback to support development

G

Goal an aim or desired result

Guided learning hours (GHL) the number of hours of direct contact required to deliver a qualification

H

Holistic the big picture; the whole qualification or curriculum

Horizontal sampling sampling across all units in the programme

I

Induction an introduction to a programme or duty

Interim QA quality assurance within the programme designed to support and develop practice

Internal quality assurance validating the integrity of the assessment

Intervention to interrupt for the purpose of resolving issues

IV Internal verifier (old terminology)

IM Internal moderator (old terminology)

IQA Internal quality assurer

L

Leading questioning posing a question (with an indicated answer contained within the question)

Learner the person being assessed by the candidate assessor

Learner journey the learner's experience of an organisation from first to final contact

LQA lead quality assurer (appointed by an approved centre)

M

Malpractice improper or negligent actions

Moderation the confirmation that marks or grades are accurate

Multilingualism speaking many languages

N

National Occupational Standards (NOS) nationally set guidelines defining the level, size and subjects used in designing units of assessment

O

Objectivity without bias

Ofqual regulatory body, Office of the Qualifications and Examinations Regulation

Open questioning posing a question designed to elicit a detailed response

P

Pathway a route; usually describing the combination of units to achieve the learner's goal

PICA acronym for components of the quality cycle; plan, implement, check, action

Plagiarism the passing off of someone else's work as your own without reference

Policy a statement of proposed actions

Portfolio a storage tool, used either paper based or electronically to collect evidence

Principle a set of values or beliefs; a rule or moral code

Procedure a way of working

Process a series of actions to meet a specific outcome

Q

Qualification a set of specifications (units of assessment) leading to an award, certificate or diploma of achievement; an accredited QCF, NQF or NVQ qualification or in-house/industry or organisationally devised set of standards used to assess the competence of trainees/learners

Qualification assessor a person accredited to assess assessor and quality assurance qualifications

Qualification quality assurer a person accredited to quality assure assessor and quality assurance qualifications

Quality assurance a system of review to confirm that processes are in place and applied to guarantee the quality of the service or product; systematic checks to provide confidence

Quality control checks on the integrity of the process

Quality improvement process to improve reliability of quality assurance systems

R

Registration an official list of entrants to a qualification

Regulation a rule or directive made by an official organisation

Reliability strategy to ensure that assessment decisions are consistent

Reliable consistently achieves the same results with different assessors and the same (or similar) group of learners

Requirements these could be the requirements of the practitioner's own organisation or those of an external organisation such as awarding organisation

Rules validity/relevance; reliability; authenticity; currency/recency; sufficiency; power of discrimination; objectivity (rules of assessment)

S

Sample a representative of the whole to show trends

Sanction a penalty for disobeying the rules

SMARTER specific, measurable, achievable, relevant, time-bounded, ethical and reviewed

SSC Sector Skills Council (part of UK Commission for Employment and Skills)

Stakeholder a person, either directly or indirectly, associated or interested in the candidate or organisation

Standards an agreed level of competence

Standardisation process to confirm decisions and create norms

Statute a written law passed by a legislative body

Subjectivity decisions influenced by other factors

Sufficient enough evidence as specified in evidence requirements or assessment strategy

Summative assessment final or summary assessment

Summative feedback feedback at the end of the unit or programme in which the final judgement is made

Summative QA quality assurance at the end of the unit or programme

T

Targets an objective or focused path towards an outcome

Testify/testimony to bear witness to; to concur; to give evidence of

Themed sampling sampling focused on a specific aspect of assessment

Trainee/Learner a person in the work place or other learning environment who is assessed by the candidate assessor

Training needs analysis (TNA) identification of required training

U

Units of assessment statements of knowledge and/or competence, clustered to make a qualification

V

Valid relevant to the standards/criteria against which the candidate is being assessed

Verification the confirmation that the processes leading to assessment decision-making are compliant, accurate and complete

Vertical sampling sampling of a single units across all assessors

W

Witness a person, other than assessor, who provides evidence of competence

References and bibliography

Printed references

Brown, R A (1992) *Portfolio development and profiling for nurses.* Lancaster: Quay Publishing Ltd

Bush, T and Middlewood, D (1997) *Managing People in Education.* London: Paul Chapman Publishing

City and Guilds (2011) *Level 3 and 4 Awards & Certificates in Assessment and Quality Assurance: qualification handbook for centres.* February 2011

City and Guilds (2009) *Level 2 Diploma in Professional Food and Beverage Service, 7103-02,* Qualification handbook, 500/7478/7. November 2009

Cole, G A and Kelly, P (2011) *Management Theory and Practice.* Andover: Cengage

Collins, D (2006) *A survival guide for college managers and leaders.* London: Continuum

Ecclestone, K (1996) *How to assess the Vocational Curriculum.* London: Kogan Page quoted in Gray, D Griffin, C and Nasta, T (2005) *Training to Teach in Further and Adult Education.* (2nd Edition) Cheltenham: Stanley Thornes

Ellis, C W (2004) *Management Skills for new Managers.* New York: AMACOM

Fautley, M and Savage, J (2008) *Assessment for Learning and Teaching in Secondary Schools.* Exeter: Learning Matters

Gardener, J (ed) (2006) *Assessment and Learning.* London: Sage

Gravells, A (2009) *Principles and practice of Assessment in the Lifelong Learning Sector.* Exeter: Learning Matters

Gray, D Griffin, C and Nasta, T (2005) *Training to Teach in Further and Adult Education.* (2nd Edition) Cheltenham: Stanley Thornes

Hill, C (2003) *Teaching using Information and Learning Technology in Further Education.* Exeter: Learning Matters

Hoyle, D (2007) *Quality Management Essentials.* Oxford: Heinemann (Elsevier)

Kolb, D (1984) *Experiential Learning: experience as a source of learning and development.* Englewood Cliffs, NJ: Prentice-Hall

LLUK (2006) *New overarching professional standards for teachers, tutors and trainers in the Lifelong Learning Sector.* November 2006. Lifelong Learning UK

O'Connell, Sir B (2005) *Creating an Outstanding College.* Cheltenham: Nelson Thornes

The Royal College of Speech and Language Therapists (2006) *Communicating Quality 3, RCSLT's guidance on best practice in service organization and provision.* London: The Royal College of Speech and Language Therapists

Walklin, L (1991) *The Assessment of Performance and Competence: a handbook for teachers and trainers.* Cheltenham: Stanley Thornes

Walklin, L (1996) *Training and Development NVQs: a handbook for FAETC candidates and NVQ trainers.* (reprinted 2001) Cheltenham: Nelson Thornes

Whalley, J, Welch, T and Williamson, L (2006). *E-Learning in FE.* London: Continuum

Wilson, L (2008) *Practical Teaching: a guide to PTLLS and CTLLS.* London: Cengage Learning

Wilson, L (2009) *Practical Teaching: a guide to PTLLS and DTLLS*. Andover: Cengage Learning

Wood, J, and Dickinson, J (2011) *Quality Assurance and Evaluation*. Exeter: Learning Matters

Web sourced references

Balancing Assessment of and for learning. Enhancement Themes – various researchers summarised on: http://www.enhancementthemes.ac.uk/themes/IntegrativeAssessment/IABalancingFeedforwardAss.asp

Award Handbook – City and Guilds: City and Guilds (2011) *Level 3 & 4 Awards & Certificates in Assessment and Quality Assurance*. www.cityandguilds.com (version 1.3 February 2011, p. 16, accessed April 2011)

City & Guilds – Enquiries and Appeals policy (August 2008): http://www.cityandguilds.com/documents/Centre%20(Generic)/Enquiries_and_Appeals_-_policy_and_procedures_V1_Dec_08(1).pdf

Code of Conduct: http://www.iebe.org.uk/index.php/code-of-conduct-for-assessors

Developing a portfolio of evidence: www.eoedeanery.nhs.uk

Equality Act: http://www.equalities.gov.uk/equality_act_2010.aspx

Equality Act: http://www.smarta.com/advice/legal/employment-law/the-equality-act-(october-1-2010)-need-to-know-for-small-businesses?gclid=CP7h7syP76cCFcoa4QodYhknaw

Investor in People: http://www.investorsinpeople.co.uk

ISO: http://www.iso.org

Matrix Assessment: http://www.matrixstandard.com

Ofqual: http://www.ofqual.gov.uk/files/Regulatory_arrangements_QCF_August08.pdf and http://www.ofqual.gov.uk/files/qca-06-2888_nvq_code_of_practice_r06.pdf

Ofsted and regional equivalents: www.ofsted.gov.uk; www.deni.gov.uk; www.hmie.gov.uk; www.estyn.gov.uk

QAA and IQER: www.qaa.ac.uk

Qualifications and Credit Framework: http://www.qcda.gov.uk/qualifications/60.aspx

Risk Assessment: http://www.hse.gov.uk/risk/fivesteps.htm

Rules of Combination: Version 4 http://www.paa-uk.org/Qualifications/Regulated/Qualifications/QCF%20Info/QCF%20 Support%20Pack/Rules%20of%20Combination%20in%20the%20QCF.pdf

Sector Skills Councils: UK Commission for Employments and Skills – http://www.ukces.org.uk/

Sector/Subject Areas: http://www.ofqual.gov.uk/files/sector_subject_areas_with_indicative_content.pdf

Total Quality Management: http://www.trainingqualitystandard.co.uk http://www.businessballs.com/dtiresources/total_quality_management_TQM.pdf

TQS Mark: withdrawn April 2011: http://www.trainingqualitystandard.co.uk

VDU Guidelines: http://www.hse.gov.uk/pubns/indg36.pdf

Vetting and Barring Scheme: www.homeoffice.gov.uk/crime/vetting-barring-scheme/

Wolf, A (2011) *Review of Vocational Education – The Wolf Report*. March 2011 https://www.education.gov.uk/publications/standard/publicationDetail/Page1/DFE-00031-2011 (accessed May 2011)

Index